China at the Threshold of a Market Economy

Michael W. Bell, Hoe Ee Khor, and Kalpana Kochhar
with Jun Ma, Simon N'guiamba, and Rajiv Lall

INTERNATIONAL MONETARY FUND
Washington DC
September 1993

Library of Congress Cataloging-in-Publication Data

Bell, Michael W.
    China at the threshold of a market economy / Michael W. Bell, Hoe
Ee Khor, and Kalpana Kochhar with Jun Ma, Simon N'guiamba, and
Rajiv Lall.
      p. cm. — (Occasional paper, ISSN 0251-6365 ; 107)
    "September 1993."
    Includes bibliographical references.
    ISBN 1-55775-349-0
    1. China—Economic policy—1976–   2. China—Economic
conditions—1976–   I. Khor, Hoe Ee. II. Kochhar, Kalpana. III. Title. IV. Series: Occasional paper (International Monetary Fund) ; no.
107.
HC427.92.B44   1993
338.951—dc20   93-34529
                                       CIP

Price: US$15.00
(US$12.00 to full-time faculty members and
students at universities and colleges)

Please send orders to:
International Monetary Fund, Publication Services
700 19th Street, N.W., Washington, D.C. 20431, U.S.A.
Tel.: (202) 623-7430   Telefax: (202) 623-7201

recycled paper

Contents

Tables

The following symbols have been used throughout this paper:

. . . to indicate that data are not available;

— to indicate that the figure is zero or less than half the final digit shown, or that the item does not exist;

– between years or months (e.g., 1991–92 or January–June) to indicate the years or months covered, including the beginning and ending years or months;

/ between years (e.g., 1991/92) to indicate a crop or fiscal (financial) year.

"Billion" means a thousand million.

Minor discrepancies between constituent figures and totals are due to rounding.

The term "country," as used in this paper, does not in all cases refer to a territorial entity that is a state as understood by international law and practice; the term also covers some territorial entities that are not states, but for which statistical data are maintained and provided internationally on a separate and independent basis.

Preface

This Occasional Paper undertakes a comprehensive review of China's reform experience since 1978. It identifies special conditions that may have affected China's capacity to implement reforms and draws implications for the direction of China's future reform strategy.

It is based on research papers prepared by the authors during 1992–93. Michael Bell, Hoe Ee Khor, Kalpana Kochhar, and Simon N'guiamba are all staff members of the IMF's Central Asia Department; Rajiv Lall is a staff member of the World Bank; and Jun Ma was a summer intern in 1992. Ms. Kochhar and Messrs. Bell and Khor integrated the material. A major part of the work on regional policies, including the statistical analyses, was carried out by Mr. Ma, while Mr. Lall and Mr. N'guiamba contributed material on the nonstate sector and China's integration into the global economy, respectively. The authors would like to thank Yusuke Horiguchi, Ichiro Otani, and Douglas Scott for valuable comments and support, and Viola Chou for research assistance. Esha Ray and Elin Knotter of the External Relations Department edited the manuscript and coordinated production of the publication.

The opinions expressed in the paper are those of the authors and should not be construed as representing the views of the IMF, its Executive Directors, or the Chinese authorities.

List of Abbreviations for China's Provinces, Municipalities, and Autonomous Regions

AH   Anhui[1]
BJ   Beijing[1]
FJ   Fujian[2]
GD   Guangdong[2]
GS   Gansu[1]

GX   Guangxi[2]
GZ   Guizhou[1]
HA   Hainan[2]
HB   Hubei[1]
HE   Henan[1]

HI   Hebei[2]
HL   Heilongjiang[3]
HN   Hunan[1]
JL   Jilin[3]
JS   Jiangsu[2]

JX   Jiangxi[1]
LN   Liaoning[2]
NM   Inner Mongolia[3]
NX   Ningxia[1]
QH   Qinghai[1]

SA   Shaanxi[1]
SC   Sichuan[1]
SD   Shandong[2]
SH   Shanghai[2]
SX   Shanxi[1]

TJ   Tianjin[2]
XJ   Xinjiang[3]
XZ   Tibet[3]
YN   Yunnan[3]
ZJ   Zhejiang[2]

---

[1]Inland.
[2]Coastal.
[3]Border.

I Overview

For three decades after the 1949 revolution, China pursued a strategy of socialist economic development based on self-reliance and the centrally directed allocation of resources to key sectors largely through administrative means. In the late 1970s, even though most political and economic institutions remained intact, China's policymakers recognized the untenability of traditional methods of economic management and began to overhaul the economic system. While maintaining the overall framework of predominant public ownership, China adopted a policy of opening up trade and investment links with the rest of the world and began to reform its domestic economic structure. In the context of these reforms, China gradually relaxed mandatory planning, decentralized economic decision making, and allowed market forces to influence an increasing number of prices. It also permitted a larger role to the nonstate sector and began transforming institutions and structures critical for the conduct of macroeconomic policy.

In large measure, the reforms proceeded without a detailed blueprint in a style that was generally incremental and experimental, in contrast with the "big bang" approach that was adopted in other former centrally planned economies of Eastern Europe and the former Soviet Union. Much of the early reform consisted of piecemeal measures involving experiments in selected sectors and regions of the country. However, over time, the contradictions generated by this partial approach led to growing acceptance by China's policymakers of the need for comprehensive reform.

This section provides an overview of the reform process, including some of its political precipitants, and a broad description of the reform phases. Section II reviews the economic conditions at the start of the reform era and examines the special features of the economic environment during the reform period. Section III discusses domestic reforms, including the recent initiatives to transform the economy to one based fully on market forces. Section IV contains a detailed presentation of the process of "opening up" to the outside world, and Section V examines the factors that influenced the performance of selected provinces as decentralization pro-

ceeded in the context of the reforms. Section VI assesses the impact of the reforms on the structure of the economy and on the degree of its integration into the world economy. It also examines the implications of the reforms for macroeconomic management and stability. Section VII contains concluding remarks.

Politics of Reform

When China initiated its reform process in 1978, it had just emerged from a major political crisis. Following the death of Mao Zedong in 1976, the ultra left faction[1] was ousted from power by a coalition of moderate forces consisting of senior veterans of the Communist Party and younger cadres that had emerged during the period of the Cultural Revolution. In the initial years, the party was led by Mao's designated successor, Hua Guofeng, who advocated minimal deviation from Maoist doctrines with regard to political and economic systems. Instead, the party concentrated its efforts on restoring political order and reviving the economy by reverting to the policies of the early 1950s. The economy was partially recentralized and the planning apparatus was strengthened. An ambitious ten-year development plan was launched, which focused on investment in heavy industry and strong reliance on imports of capital equipment. Within two years, however, the plan was aborted because of serious balance of payments difficulties resulting from a strong surge in imports of capital goods.

By late 1978, reformist views, spearheaded by Deng Xiaoping, had become dominant in the party. At the Third Plenum of the Central Committee of the Communist Party in December 1978, the leadership made a decisive break with the legacy of the Cultural Revolution and resolved to focus the party's work on economic development. The principal contradiction in China was identified as the backwardness of the economy in responding to the needs of the people. Accordingly, the principal task of the party was defined as developing the productive

---

[1] Popularly referred to as the "gang of four."

1

forces of the population.[2] To this end, the new leadership set out to reform those aspects of the economic system that had impeded the development of the economy.

However, although the new leadership was agreed on the need to break with the past and to reform the economic system, there was no unanimity in views on the pace and nature of reform, particularly the role of the market versus that of planning in a socialist economy. Conservatives favored retaining a central role for planning in a reformed economic system, whereas the more radical elements envisaged a greatly diminished and reformed role for planning. In the early years, such differences of views were of little political import as the reforms adopted then were experimental and partial, directed mainly at rejuvenating an economy that had become moribund as a result of years of political interference combined with the diminishing effectiveness of administrative planning. However, as the reforms began to spread across the economy, the inadequacy of a partial approach became increasingly apparent as manifested in the periodic outbreaks of macroeconomic instability. Consequently, as a more comprehensive approach to reforms became imperative, the differences in views began to bear directly on the direction and substance of policies, resulting in periodic shifts in the emphasis of policy. Despite occasional setbacks, however, the more radical views prevailed during most of the post-1978 period. In 1992, a decisive ideological change occurred when the party embraced the views of senior leader Deng Xiaoping and called for the establishment of a socialist market economy.

Evolution of Conceptual Framework

Although China has successfully pursued a strategy of reform and opening up of its economy for 15 years, the reforms have not derived from any comprehensive blueprint. In general, the reform measures were first introduced on an experimental basis in some localities—often as a result of local initiatives—and were adopted on a national scale only when they had proved successful at the local level. This pragmatic approach to reforms helped to avoid major economic disruptions and to transform the economy from a predominantly central planning system to one in which market mechanisms play an important role.[3]

An important ideological issue that has permeated the reform process is the nature of a market system and whether such a system is consistent with socialism; the role of planning is a corollary issue. In the initial phase of the reform process, the issue was resolved by viewing the market as a useful supplement to a predominantly planned economy.[4] In the mid-1980s, the role of the market was elevated when the goal of economic reforms was stated as the establishment of a "socialist planned commodity economy." In this formulation, China was considered to be at a primitive stage of socialism in which the commodity economy was an essential part. Hence, the objective of reform was to establish an economic system that combined planning with the use of market forces.[5]

It is in this context that the importance of the resolution of the Fourteenth Party Congress to establish a "socialist market economy" should be seen. The party summed up the experience of the previous 15 years and embraced Deng Xiaoping's argument that the market mechanism is merely an instrument of economic development and not a defining characteristic of a social system; the socialist character of the economy is preserved by the predominant ownership of the public sector (including the state and the collectives[6]) over the means of production. The market system is therefore fully compatible with either capitalist or socialist systems. Under the new paradigm, the aim of reform is to establish an economic structure in which market forces, under the macroeconomic influence of the state, will determine relative prices and the allocation of resources. The new paradigm is an important ideological breakthrough because it eliminates the ambivalence of the leadership over the direction of reform and allows for bolder policies to be undertaken to achieve the stated goal of establishing a market economy.

Phases of Reform

The economic reforms in China may conveniently be viewed as unfolding in several phases: the first

---

[2]Under Mao, the principal contradiction had been defined as the continuing struggle between classes, and hence the main task of the party was to continue the revolutionary struggle.

[3]The pragmatic approach embodies the principle of "seeking truth from facts" and has been described as "crossing the river by feeling the stones under the feet."

[4]This perception of the relation between planning and the market is often described as the "bird in the cage" theory, which was propounded by party veteran Chen Yun. In this metaphor, the market is the bird and the plan is the cage. The cage can be enlarged to give greater freedom to the bird, but without the cage, the bird will fly away—which is analogous to disorder in the market.

[5]In this view, the relation between the state and the market is captured by the expression "the State controls the market, the market guides the enterprises." For an elaboration of the theoretical framework, see Zhao Ziyang (1987).

[6]Collectives are basically communities at the level of the village or township or a neighborhood in an urban area.

phase spanned the period 1978–84; the second phase, 1984–88; the third covered 1988–91; and the fourth began in 1992. In the early stages, reform efforts focused on rejuvenating the economy and overcoming the adverse effects of key Maoist doctrines that had been the guiding principles of economic policies during the greater part of the 25 years preceding reforms. In the view of the leadership, the main factors retarding the development of the economy were (1) a deep distrust of the market system; (2) egalitarianism and reliance on collective efforts with their invidious effects on individual work incentives; and (3) a policy of extreme self-reliance bordering on autarky at all levels from the national to the provincial and commune. Although Mao had held a deep aversion to bureaucracy, his suspicion of the market system left the dilemma of how to coordinate myriad activities to maintain macroeconomic balance. He had sought to resolve this by decentralizing the administrative system of planning and advocating self-reliance at the local level. Private initiative was tolerated but highly regulated.

First Phase (1978–84)

Initially, the policies pursued were similar to those adopted in the early 1960s to rehabilitate the economy in the aftermath of the Great Leap Forward.[7] These policies placed greater emphasis on material incentives and allowed a larger role for the market. In particular, procurement prices of agricultural products were increased, the diversification and specialization of crops were encouraged, restrictions on rural markets (trade fairs) were relaxed, and the organization of farming was decentralized from the collective to the household level. In industry, the bonus system was reinstituted, the retention of depreciation allowance was permitted, and experimentation began on profit retention by state-owned enterprises. In foreign economic relations, preferential policies were conferred on special economic zones with the aim of attracting foreign investment and technology, promoting exports, and having them act as laboratories for bolder market-oriented reforms.

Second Phase (1984–88)

The success of the initial rural reforms emboldened the authorities to adopt a wide-ranging set of measures to reform the urban industrial sectors in 1984. These measures included the establishment of a two-track pricing system; the introduction of enterprise taxation; the reform of the wage system to establish a closer link between remuneration and

productivity; and the breakup of the monobank system leading to the establishment of a central bank. The investment system was reformed to encourage enterprises to borrow from the banking system to finance projects rather than relying on the state as in the past. The revenue-sharing system between the central and local governments was revised to allow for greater retention of revenue by the latter. To attract more capital and technical know-how, 14 major cities in the coastal areas were opened up to foreign trade and investment. In 1986, many of these measures were revised and expanded. These included establishing swap centers for trading of retained foreign exchange earnings, decentralizing trade through the establishment of local foreign trade corporations, and adopting a contract responsibility system for enterprises similar to that in agriculture.

Third Phase (1988–91)

The period from mid-1988 to 1991 represented a period of retrenchment. The reforms adopted were successful in spurring demand and production, which led to rising inflation, and by early 1988 the annual inflation rate reached double-digit levels. The plans for a new round of price reforms were deferred, and there was some reversal of earlier reforms as price controls were recentralized under a "rectification program" during which the authorities took strong measures to cool the overheated economy. The retrenchment measures succeeded in stabilizing prices, but they also resulted in a sharp slowdown in the economy, particularly in the industrial sector. As a result, losses of state-owned enterprises mounted, interenterprise debt escalated, and inventories accumulated, threatening to destabilize the macroeconomic situation. To avert a looming economic crisis, in late 1990, the authorities resorted to stimulative monetary and investment policies to reactivate the economy. Reflecting the change in policy stance, the economy began to recover in 1991. During this latter period, the authorities took advantage of generally stable prices to make substantial realignments in relative prices and to liberalize certain prices.

Fourth Phase (1992–Present)

In early 1992, the authorities declared an end to the rectification program and announced their intention to accelerate the process of reform and opening up. The process culminated in October 1992 when the Communist Party formally embraced paramount leader Deng Xiaoping's view that the market system was not incompatible with the ideals of socialism and called for the establishment of a socialist market

---

[7]See Riskin (1987).

economy. The new paradigm represents an important ideological breakthrough and has paved the way for the authorities to begin to formulate comprehensive plans to establish a fully market-based economy. In March 1992, the country's constitution was amended to delete references to a planned economy and to enshrine the new goal of establishing a market system. Other important initiatives included an acceleration of the work program to develop a legal and regulatory framework to support a market economy, the decision to undertake a major restructuring of the role and functions of government, and plans to speed up enterprise, financial, and social reforms.

Salient Features of the Chinese Approach to Reform

The reform process in China has often been characterized as gradual and incremental, in contrast with the reforms undertaken in countries in Eastern Europe and the former Soviet Union. This probably arises from the different political circumstances of these countries at the time the economic reforms were initiated. As mentioned above, although there was a political crisis just two years prior to the inception of reforms in China, the Communist Party had remained intact, and a powerful coalition had emerged within the party that was united in wishing to undertake economic reforms with the ultimate aim of developing China into a modern socialist state. In other words, the goal of the Chinese leadership was not to transform the entire political economic system but to develop the Chinese economy as rapidly as possible within the basic framework of socialism and the existing political system.

What are some of the salient characteristics of the reforms undertaken during the past 15 years? In general, the reforms were undertaken first on an experimental basis in some localities before they were applied to the whole country. In the view of China's policymakers, this gradual approach to reform had several advantages. First, major disruptions to the economy were avoided, and in case the policies turned out to be deficient, they could be modified to suit national and local conditions. Second, by implementing first those policies that were likely to be successful, the leadership was able to build up political support for further reform. This was particularly important in avoiding social unrest and political conflicts that could derail the whole reform process. Third, for certain reforms to be effective, it was necessary to build new institutions, to set up new legal and regulatory frameworks, and to train personnel to become familiar with the new practices, all of which are time-consuming tasks. Fourth, the administrative apparatus of the planning

system would continue to be available—albeit with diminishing effectiveness—until a new system could become effective.

Another important feature of the reforms was the use of intermediate mechanisms to smooth the transition between two different economic systems to avoid major disruptions that could result from an abrupt shift from one system to another. Specific examples included establishing a dual-track pricing system to improve the allocation of resources at the margin; establishing a swap market in foreign exchange retention rights to improve the use of foreign exchange; setting up open economic zones to introduce foreign capital and technology to China; using the contract responsibility system to encourage behavior by economic agents that is closer to that of the market; authorizing some local governments to enact and experiment with market-oriented legislation; and decentralizing decisions to motivate officials at the local level. The use of intermediate mechanisms can be seen as a way of encouraging economic agents to adapt their behavior prior to the eventual phasing out of the planning system. Moreover, because the reforms were interconnected, for any one measure to be fully effective, it would be essential to implement all reforms simultaneously—an impracticable task given the limited experience and knowledge available in China. For instance, to establish a fully market-determined exchange rate, it is necessary to rationalize the price structure, to harden the budget constraint of enterprises, to commercialize the state-owned banks, and so forth.

A distinguishing feature of the Chinese reforms is the attempt by the leadership to preserve the socialist character of the economy. As such, the authorities have not pursued a strategy of mass privatization as in some of the transitional economies of Eastern Europe and the former Soviet Union. However, any constraint this might have imposed on reform has been diminished by limiting the concept of socialism to the dominance of public ownership and control of strategic sectors in the economy, supplemented by nonstate and private ownership. The modified definition has allowed the authorities considerable leeway in implementing policies that promote the development of the market system, such as the use of material incentives. The household responsibility system in agriculture is one example. Although land continues to be publicly owned, its use and management is contracted out to individual households. The emphasis on "ownership" has allowed the authorities to implement changes to the "operating mechanism" of state-owned enterprises (SOEs) to sever the close links between these and the state, particularly with respect to their finances and management, with the aim of transforming them into autonomous units responsible for their own profits and losses.[8] Another important aspect of the new framework is the highly successful policy to promote the development of the nonstate sector. This sector is defined to include collective enterprises, individual and private businesses, foreign-funded enterprises, and joint-ownership enterprises. The rapid growth of the non-state sector has strengthened the economy and has facilitated efforts to transform the traditional state sector.

A major concomitant of the market-oriented reforms to date is the progressive decentralization of economic decision making. Indeed, to a significant extent, this decentralization has stimulated some aspects of the reform process—notably in agriculture and the external sector—although it has also complicated other aspects, in particular the implementation of demand management through indirect means in a more market-oriented setting. Although decentralization was a recurrent theme during the pre-reform period, the more recent process is distinguished from the past by its depth and extensiveness, as well as the fact that it has been combined with the use of market mechanisms. Over the years, the administrative apparatus of planning had been devolved to the local authorities, but decentralization since 1978 has gone far beyond that by severing the ties between the economic agents and the state, by allowing economic agents to base their decisions on market signals, and by conferring considerable autonomy in resource allocation on the local governments. This has become a self-sustaining process as local authorities have used their growing autonomy to strengthen their hand in negotiations over resource-sharing with the center and in taking initiatives in such areas as investment.

An important consequence of the partial approach to reform so far has been the tendency for the economy to experience "stop-go" cycles of macroeconomic instability as the authorities have relinquished direct control over the economy, while indirect instruments have remained ineffective because of the incompleteness of reforms. As decentralization has proceeded, the traditional administrative system of macroeconomic control has become less effective as local authorities and state-owned enterprises have gained greater autonomy to pursue their narrow objectives of promoting growth and development within a relatively weak framework of financial discipline. As a result, macroeconomic instability has tended to become more severe with each cycle. So far the authorities have managed to regain control of the economy on each occasion by combining economic policy actions with direct administrative intervention. However, such an approach has become increasingly risky as is evident from the last episode in 1988–91. The task of maintaining macroeconomic stability is likely to remain one of the key challenges ahead even as the authorities take steps to establish a more effective system of macroeconomic management in the latest phase of reforms.

---

[8]Section III elaborates on enterprise reforms to date.

II Initial Conditions and Special Characteristics of Chinese Reform

This section reviews some of the economic conditions at the start of the reform era and certain characteristics of the economic environment during the period. It highlights a number of special features of the Chinese reform process that may be germane to understanding its impact and compares China's experience with those of other former centrally planned economies in transition.

Initial Conditions and Reform Environment

Macroeconomic and Structural Conditions

The Soviet-style "command" economy model was first chosen to guide the development strategy following the establishment of the People's Republic of China in 1949, but in time Chinese leaders became increasingly disenchanted with some aspects of this model, particularly the high degree of centralization. The central planning apparatus was overhauled in 1957; the central government retained control over important large- and medium-scale industrial enterprises but for other enterprises, particularly those engaged in light manufacturing, control was transferred to local authorities. Although there were periods before 1978 when central control was tightened and then loosened again, China never returned to being centrally planned to the same degree as the former Soviet Union or some Central and East European countries.

What was the economic legacy of the development strategy pursued in the two and a half decades up to 1978? Despite the depression and famine following the Great Leap Forward (1958–59) and the political upheavals of the Cultural Revolution, China had achieved growth rates averaging 6 percent a year between 1952 and 1978 (Table 1), albeit with significant variability. Measured inflation was for the most part low, and government budget deficits and external imbalances were rarely large. Measured in terms of the production of electric power, cement, and steel, China's industrial base in the late 1970s was comparable to that of Japan and the Soviet Union in the 1960s, and its record on income distribution and on social indicators compared favorably with those of middle-income countries. Reflecting an aversion to foreign borrowing in the three decades up to 1978, China entered the reform period with virtually no external debt.[9] This stood in contrast to other developing countries in Eastern Europe and elsewhere where relatively heavy external borrowing was used primarily to finance consumption and inefficient investment (Table 2). In short, the Chinese economy, unlike those of other former centrally planned economies in transition, was not in a deep crisis of macroeconomic instability just before reforms were implemented. Thus, the question arises as to the factors that provided the impetus for economic reforms and their scope.

Although no crisis was apparent at the macroeconomic level, there was growing discontent with the system, especially in the rural areas. The recorded economic growth prior to 1978 was achieved largely by increasing the amounts of labor and capital employed, with little or no growth in total factor productivity. Moreover, there were sharp swings in output growth associated primarily with the waves of centralization and decentralization. The economy faced chronic and fundamental economic difficulties, many similar to those encountered by other centrally planned economies, including a distorted pricing system, inefficient resource allocation, concentration of investment in heavy industry at the expense of basic infrastructure and the resultant bottlenecks, stagnation in agricultural production with shortages of nongrain products, isolation from foreign competition, a pervasive emphasis on quantity rather than on quality, and slow growth in per capita consumption with acute shortages of many consumer goods and housing.

China's economic growth during the 1960s and the first half of the 1970s was much lower than several of its East Asian neighbors (Table 3). Moreover, owing to the essentially autarkic regime of the previous three decades, China had made little technological progress in many critical areas. Chinese

---

[9]The total stock of debt in 1978 is estimated to have been 12 percent of exports (see Cheng (1982)).

Table 1. Selected Macroeconomic Indicators
(Annual percent change, unless otherwise specified)

	Real Net Material Product[1]	General Retail Prices	Government Budget Balance[2]	Exports[3]	Imports[3]	Trade Balance[3]
1952	...	...	1.3	0.8	1.1	−0.3
1953	14.0	3.4	0.4	1.0	1.4	−0.4
1954	5.8	2.3	2.2	1.1	1.3	−0.2
1955	6.4	1.0	0.3	1.4	1.7	−0.3
1956	14.1	—	−0.2	1.6	1.6	—
1957	4.5	1.5	0.7	1.6	1.5	0.1
1958	22.0	0.2	−1.9	2.0	1.9	0.1
1959	8.2	0.9	−5.3	2.3	2.1	0.2
1960	−1.4	3.1	−6.7	1.9	2.0	−0.1
1961	−29.7	16.2	−1.1	1.5	1.5	—
1962	−6.5	3.8	0.9	1.5	1.2	0.3
1963	10.7	−5.9	0.3	1.6	1.3	0.3
1964	16.5	−3.7	—	1.9	1.5	0.4
1965	16.9	−2.7	0.5	2.2	2.0	0.2
1966	17.0	−0.3	1.0	2.4	2.2	0.2
1967	−7.2	−0.7	−1.5	2.1	2.0	0.1
1968	−6.5	0.1	0.1	2.1	2.0	0.1
1969	19.3	−1.1	—	2.2	1.8	0.4
1970	23.3	−0.2	0.7	2.3	2.3	—
1971	7.0	−0.8	0.6	2.6	2.2	0.4
1972	2.9	−0.2	—	3.4	2.9	0.5
1973	8.3	0.6	—	5.8	5.2	0.6
1974	1.1	0.5	−0.3	6.9	7.6	−0.7
1975	8.3	0.2	−0.2	7.3	7.5	−0.2
1976	−2.7	0.3	−1.2	6.9	6.6	0.3
1977	7.8	2.0	1.1	7.6	7.2	0.4
1978	11.7	0.7	0.3	9.8	10.9	−1.1
1979	7.6	2.0	−5.1	13.7	15.7	−2.0
1980	7.9	6.0	−3.5	18.1	20.0	−1.9
1981	4.4	2.4	−0.6	22.0	22.0	—
1982	8.8	1.9	−0.7	22.3	19.3	3.0
1983	10.4	1.5	−0.9	22.2	21.4	0.8
1984	14.7	2.8	−0.8	26.1	27.4	−1.3
1985	12.8	8.8	0.3	27.4	42.2	−14.8
1986	8.1	6.0	−0.9	30.9	42.9	−12.0
1987	10.9	7.3	−0.9	39.4	43.2	−3.8
1988	11.3	18.6	−0.7	47.5	55.2	−7.7
1989	4.4	17.8	−0.7	52.5	59.1	−6.6
1990	4.1	2.1	−1.0	62.1	53.4	8.7
1991	7.7	2.7	−0.8	71.9	63.8	8.1
1992	13.0	5.3	−1.0	85.0	80.6	4.4

Source: China Statistical Yearbook, 1992.
[1] From 1978, the series is gross national product.
[2] Revenue minus expenditure on the basis of the authorities' definitions in percent of net material product or gross national product.
[3] In billions of U.S. dollars, on a customs basis.

leaders increasingly recognized that unless the technological disparity between China and her neighbors was effectively addressed, these output gaps would only widen.

Domestic Saving

A key factor in the successful transformation of economies is the availability of resources for non-inflationary financing of adjustment and growth. Since the inception of reforms, China has enjoyed high rates of domestic savings—estimated at 30–35 percent.[10] These rates are considerably higher than

[10] These figures should be treated with some caution as serious conceptual and practical problems exist in measuring savings in China.

Table 2. Selected Countries: Debt and Debt-Service Indicators

	1980	1986	1987	1988	1989	1990	1991
External debt as a ratio to GNP							
China	1.5	8.5	11.6	11.3	10.7	14.2	16.4
Argentina	48.4	70.5	76.4	66.5	119.1	62.3	49.2
Brazil	31.2	43.7	42.3	34.3	25.6	25.2	28.8
Former Czechoslovakia	...	12.0	12.8	14.4	15.7	18.6	29.5
Hungary	44.8	74.0	77.9	69.5	73.7	67.6	77.0
India	11.9	21.3	22.0	21.7	23.9	23.7	29.2
Indonesia	28.0	52.2	69.0	64.3	59.7	66.1	66.4
Korea	48.7	45.5	31.0	21.1	15.6	14.4	14.4
Malaysia	28.0	86.5	80.4	61.6	50.5	44.6	47.6
Mexico	30.5	82.5	82.1	61.4	48.5	41.7	36.9
Poland	...	51.5	69.9	63.9	54.6	82.0	61.4
Thailand	26.0	45.4	42.4	37.0	34.4	35.0	39.1
Debt-service ratios							
China	4.4	9.6	9.5	9.7	11.4	11.4	12.0
Argentina	37.3	76.2	74.3	44.5	36.2	39.4	48.1
Brazil	63.1	47.0	41.9	48.2	34.6	22.6	30.8
Former Czechoslovakia	...	8.0	7.9	8.8	9.6	10.0	11.5
Hungary	18.9	41.0	33.5	31.1	29.7	34.3	32.5
India	9.3	32.0	29.4	30.3	27.6	28.3	30.6
Indonesia	13.9	37.4	37.1	40.4	35.5	31.1	33.0
Korea	19.7	26.7	32.3	14.8	11.8	10.7	...
Malaysia	6.3	22.2	21.1	24.7	15.6	11.2	8.4
Mexico	49.5	54.2	40.1	48.0	37.9	27.8	30.9
Poland	...	12.8	14.2	10.6	9.4	4.9	5.4
Thailand	18.9	30.1	22.0	20.2	16.3	17.0	13.1

Source: World Bank, *World Debt Tables*, 1992–93.

in most developing countries and even industrial countries, and are only slightly lower than in countries like Japan and Singapore. In addition to an increase in the saving rate, the most notable trend since the early 1980s has been a shift in the composition of total saving from the state sector to households. In particular, the share of household saving in total saving as well as in total household income has risen sharply since 1979. Household saving is estimated to have accounted for about 40 percent of domestic savings in 1991. Further, rural households accounted for an estimated 75 percent of total household saving. There can be no doubt that the high savings rate contributed to China's success in maintaining macroeconomic balance during the reform period.

From a policy perspective, the issue of interest is whether the high saving rate reflects a behavioral characteristic of Chinese households or is merely a monetary phenomenon, that is, "involuntary or forced saving" as a result of repressed inflation. Clearly, the two have very different policy implications. If the magnitude of repressed inflation is small, the danger of a sharp rise in inflation following price liberalization should be limited.

Several arguments can be made in favor of each side of this issue. For example, it can be argued that, until recently, significant price controls existed in the economy. This, together with the rapid monetary expansion that has taken place, has led to an increased degree of forced savings in the economy. Furthermore, as the state continues to provide for retirement, education, housing, and health care, most of the theoretical reasons underlying the choice to save are not relevant in China.

On the other hand, it could also be argued that with the emergence of the two-track pricing system in China—under which individuals and enterprises are free to buy goods at market-related prices at the margin—money holdings or savings cannot be considered "involuntary." Moreover, unlike urban households for which enterprises provide housing, medical care, and pensions, rural households have to rely on their own savings to procure these services. Another reason for high rural saving is their access to lucrative investment opportunities, par-

Table 3. Selected Economies: Growth Rates of GNP and GNP Per Capita, 1960–76
(Annual percent change)

	GNP	GNP Per Capita
Korea	9.6	7.3
Singapore	9.5	7.5
Japan	9.1	8.0
Taiwan Province of China	9.0	6.2
Hong Kong	8.7	6.4
Thailand	7.7	4.6
Malaysia	6.7	3.9
Pakistan	6.1	3.2
China	5.7	3.6
Philippines	5.4	2.4
Indonesia	5.2	3.1
India	3.5	1.2
Myanmar	2.9	0.7

Sources: World Bank, *World Bank Atlas, 1978*; and *China Statistical Yearbook, 1991*.

ticularly since the introduction of the household responsibility system and the easing of restrictions on nonagricultural activities. Urban households in contrast have had little portfolio choice (until very recently) outside bank saving deposits.

Empirical studies[11] on the nature of households' decision making with respect to saving in China have been far from conclusive on whether and to what extent saving is "involuntary." Some studies, such as Dessi (1991) based on sample survey responses, have concluded that forced saving is significant among urban households and could account for as much as 15–25 percent of urban household saving. On the other hand, there appears to be much less evidence that rural saving is involuntary.

Access to External Financing

Even with greater willingness to turn to foreign sources to finance its modernization and development process, China's policy toward external borrowing has been relatively conservative. Borrowing has remained predominantly medium and long term from official sources, and a substantial proportion of

[11]Feltenstein, Lebow, and van Wijnbergen (1990) find evidence for the existence of "forced" savings in China, whereas Qian (1988) concludes that the data do not reject the hypothesis that the high savings rates are the result of structural and behavioral shifts and do not represent involuntary saving.

it has been on concessional terms. In absolute terms, China's external debt did increase dramatically, rising tenfold in the 1980s. In particular, the rapid economic growth and import liberalization of the mid-1980s was accompanied by a surge in external indebtedness, with the share of short-term commercial debt rising sharply.

However, prudent debt management and an improved monitoring capability have served to limit the ratio of total debt outstanding to GNP to about 16 percent in 1992, with about 20 percent of total debt being on concessional terms. Throughout the reform period, China's debt-service ratio has remained much lower than in most other developing countries. Although in the immediate wake of the events of June 1989 China's access to the market for medium- and long-term funds became tight, there appears to have been no enduring impact on creditworthiness as the external accounts strengthened and reform reappeared on the agenda.

In addition, China has had considerable success in attracting foreign direct investment, which increased from less than $400 million in 1982 to over $11 billion in 1992. In this regard, the special roles played by Hong Kong and, more recently, Taiwan Province of China are noteworthy. Between 1988 and 1992, Hong Kong alone accounted for more than two-thirds of foreign direct investment inflows to China, the major part being absorbed by the coastal province of Guangdong. Since 1990, investment from Taiwan Province of China has also been increasing, particularly in Fujian. These trends are no doubt largely attributable to the cultural and geographic proximity of these territories to China.

Openness of the Economy

In the pre-reform period, the overriding preoccupation with self-sufficiency resulted in the development of domestic oil production, which in turn served to insulate the Chinese economy from the effects of two oil shocks in the 1970s. Also, through much of the pre-reform period and even the early reform years, China remained a relatively closed economy, with imports and exports as a ratio to GNP being less than 10 percent in 1978 and remaining below 20 percent until 1984. As a result, the economy was less vulnerable to external disturbances such as recessions in world markets and fluctuations in interest rates. Moreover, the absence of bilateral payments arrangements, such as the Council for Mutual Economic Assistance (CMEA), helped prevent the emergence of further distortions and rigidities in the trade system in addition to those generated by the pricing system and the strict administrative control of external trade and payments, and served to expose Chinese exporters to some competition.

Special Characteristics of Reform

Regional Policy

China has adopted a selective approach under which certain provinces or regions were chosen to play a leading role in the reform process. This approach partly reflected a strong predilection for experimentation arising from the authorities' perception of the complexity of simultaneous nation-wide reform in such a large country, and their concern with avoiding instability. A persistent theme of the reforms was a gradually increasing outward orientation ("opening to the outside world"), under which China attempted to increase its foreign exchange earning capacity. A further characteristic of the early reforms was their focus in regions with a relatively low proportion of large state-owned enterprises subject to mandatory planning.

These features led to the emergence of the coastal provinces as the focal point of many aspects of the reform effort to the extent that they proved a driving force behind the reform process. It might also be argued that the reform process merely removed the impediments to the coastal provinces' exploiting their comparative advantages. The first step was to establish the special economic zones (SEZs),[12] giving them more financial and administrative powers, including the right to approve large-scale investment projects, to grant tax concessions and other incentives to foreign-funded enterprises, and, until recently, to retain a higher proportion of foreign exchange. As the positive results of these experiments became evident, the approach was extended to a number of other "coastal open cities," each of which acquired the right to offer incentives to potential investors, allowing a degree of competition among localities and potential for divergence in economic performance among provinces or regions. Indeed, it might be observed that in a number of instances the localities, "given an inch, have taken a mile."

Two by-products of these developments were a growing disparity in economic growth among provinces and pressure from the provinces for greater autonomy in their economic relations with the central government, particularly in matters affecting resource allocation. Net transfers between the provinces and the center have been governed by contracts of three to four years' duration, and a perception remains that these transfers are not equitable. Moreover, since the major part of the state's revenue is retained in the provinces, the center's ability to undertake macroeconomic management through fiscal policy is diminished. This is exacerbated by the difficulty faced by the People's Bank of China to contain credit expansion because of local political pressure on provincial branches of banks.

Decentralization and its Effects

The Chinese reform process has been characterized by the progressive decentralization of economic decision-making power. Nowhere is the process of devolution of decision-making powers and control from the center to the provinces more apparent than in the change that has taken place in the system of state investment and allocation of raw materials through the material supply system. Before reforms were initiated, these systems were at the heart of Chinese central planning. Central government control over both the level and composition of investment has declined significantly. Furthermore, state control over the allocation of key raw materials has steadily been eroded with the progressive reduction in the scope of mandatory planning.

Under these circumstances, China's policymakers are faced with two major issues (dealt with in greater detail in Section V below). First, with the decline in the central government's direct authority over investment decisions, the need for effective indirect macroeconomic policy levers with which to regulate the overall level of investment demand has become critical. Second, the potential for conflict between central and local investment priorities now exists, largely owing to (1) the distortions in the price system, which make investments in priority sectors such as energy and transportation infrastructure unattractive to provincial and local authorities; and (2) underdeveloped capital markets that blunt financial intermediation, with investible surpluses tending to be reinvested in the areas from which they originate irrespective of rates of return in other provinces. The latter has led to the wasteful duplication of investments across provinces and investments that are less than optimal.[13]

The share of investment in China's GDP has always been high, underscoring the reliance placed by the authorities on "accumulation" for growth. In the pre-reform period, most fixed asset investment was under central control. Total fixed asset investment consisted of investment by state-owned enterprises, collectives, and individuals.[14] These investments

---

[12]The process of opening up is described more fully in Section IV below.

[13]See Singh (1992) for a more detailed discussion of these problems.

[14]Investment by SOEs is further subdivided into capital construction—involving the construction of new facilities and the expansion of capacity; technical transformation and updating—aimed at modifying and upgrading existing facilities; and other investment, mainly oil and mineral exploration.

Table 4. Total Fixed Asset Investment
(In percent of total, unless otherwise specified)

	1981	1985	1987	1988	1989	1990	1991
Total fixed asset investment	100.0	100.0	100.0	100.0	100.0	100.0	100.0
By ownership							
State-owned units	66.1	66.1	63.1	61.4	61.3	65.6	65.9
Collectively owned units	16.8	12.9	15.0	15.8	13.8	11.9	12.7
Individual	17.1	21.0	21.9	22.7	24.9	22.5	21.5
By source of finance							
State budget	28.4	16.0	13.1	9.1	8.3	8.7	6.8
Domestic loans	...	20.1	23.0	20.6	17.3	19.6	23.5
Foreign investment	...	3.6	4.8	5.8	6.6	6.2	5.7
Self-raised funds	71.6[1]	60.3	47.9	64.5	56.9	52.3	52.3
Others	...	...	11.2	...	10.9	13.1	11.8

Source: *China Statistical Yearbook*, 1991.
[1] Includes all other forms of financing outside the state budget.

were financed primarily through the budget or under the credit plan through policy loans from the specialized banks. The central government could therefore closely regulate the level of investment and its composition. Although most investment decisions continue to be made by some level of government after the initiation of reforms,[15] the share of total investment financed through direct budgetary appropriations has declined dramatically (Table 4). To some extent, this reduction is not surprising given the rapid growth of the nonstate sector in China over the past few years. However, similar trends are discernible even when the share of funds from the budget in investment by state-owned units is examined (Table 5).

The principal factor accounting for the decline in the share of investment financed through the budget is the sharp decrease in budgetary revenues, from the equivalent of 27 percent of GNP in 1979 to 16 percent in 1992. The fall in revenues is, in turn, attributable to the structural weaknesses in a transitional revenue system marked by ad hoc contracts between the state and the enterprises, and between central and local governments (see Section V for a

more detailed discussion of these arrangements). With these decentralized arrangements, local authorities have the incentive to collect fewer taxes that must be shared with or turned over to the center. Resources are thus kept in the hands of enterprises through generous local tax exemptions. "Voluntary" contributions from enterprises have left growing amounts of surplus funds in the hands of local governments—"extrabudgetary funds"—which have been used to finance local investment initiatives. As will be discussed below in Section VI, each phase of China's reforms has been accompanied by a surge in aggregate demand—primarily investment demand. This fact, together with the diminution of central authorities' influence over the level and composition of investment, has had important implications for the stability of the macroeconomic situation during the phases of reform, and indeed for the pace of the reform itself.

Enterprise Ownership

A key question that has faced economic reformers in China, as elsewhere, is whether the continuation of public ownership represents an insuperable barrier to the functioning of markets and efficient resource allocation. China has consistently maintained its preference for public ownership as a means of achieving its vision of a socialist market economy. As envisaged by China's policymakers, such a system would be characterized by increased competition and the elimination of mandatory planning, but not necessarily by the replacement of state ownership with "private" ownership, as in a capitalist

---

[15] Generally speaking, large infrastructure projects and major investments in key SOEs are approved and financed by the central government. Smaller infrastructure projects and investments by medium- and small-scale SOEs are authorized by provincial and local authorities. Finally, investments that are outside the plan are largely undertaken by the collective and the township and village enterprise (TVE) sector. The latter are financed mainly from bank loans and the retained earnings of enterprises.

Table 5. Fixed Asset Investment of State-Owned Enterprises
(In percent of total, unless otherwise specified)

	1985	1987	1988	1989	1990	1991
Total investment	100.0	100.0	100.0	100.0	100.0	100.0
By source of finance						
State budget	24.0	20.5	14.7	13.4	13.2	10.2
Domestic loans	23.0	24.5	24.2	20.9	23.6	28.1
Foreign investment	5.3	7.3	9.0	10.1	9.1	8.4
Self-raised funds	47.7	47.6	52.2	55.6	54.1	53.4
By sector						
Agriculture	2.7	2.4	2.3	2.4	2.7	2.8
Industry	54.4	61.2	62.5	63.0	62.0	58.2
o/w: Energy	21.8	23.6	23.3	27.9	29.0	26.4
Transportation and communications	13.5	12.3	11.5	10.7	11.9	13.4

Source: *China Statistical Yearbook*, 1991.

system. The objective is to retain the predominance of public ownership supplemented by nonstate and private ownership, while achieving an effective separation between state ownership and control of enterprises. Although the development of a socialist market economy is a recent goal—marking an important change in the ideology of economic reform in China—throughout the reform process ownership structures have been modified in a number of important respects that had major implications for enterprise management. In particular, these modifications might be viewed as an attempt to simulate market conditions by encouraging profit-maximizing behavior.

First, there was a substantial degree of decentralization in control from the central government to provincial and municipal governments, notably in foreign trade. In some respects, the size and complexity of the structure of the Chinese Government may have facilitated the effective decentralization of control. The significance of this change is that although government interference has not been eliminated, lower levels of government view enterprises under their jurisdiction as a source of revenue and have therefore been willing to allow relatively free rein to profit-maximizing behavior.

Second, the introduction of the household responsibility system and the lifting of restrictions on nonfarm activities in rural areas led to the rapid growth of various forms of enterprises—notably the TVEs—that fall almost entirely outside the jurisdiction of state or provincial authorities. They are not subject to state planning norms, price setting, or other forms of state intervention; conversely, they do not have preferential access to credit or material supplies, nor do they benefit from investment from the central

government or from guaranteed sales to the state. That is, these enterprises operate largely in a market-oriented manner, facing a highly competitive environment and hard budget constraints. See Box 1 for further details on China's nonstate industrial sector.

Third, the initiatives to open up parts of the economy to foreign trade and investment led to the emergence of various forms of private and quasi-private ownership, both domestic and foreign, through the establishment of foreign-funded enterprises (FFEs). In addition, the Government has encouraged private entrepreneurship in some areas of the economy, particularly in the service and commerce sectors. Even in the industrial sector, the share of privately owned enterprises in industrial output tripled to over 5 percent in the five years through 1990. Private share ownership is still limited in scope, although with recent moves to open securities exchanges, private shareholding of state-owned companies can be expected to increase.

Fourth, even among the enterprises that remain under state control, the scope for direct intervention has gradually eroded as mandatory planning has been reduced, price setting powers devolved, more autonomy in investment decisions allowed, and higher profit retention permitted. Also, in the mid-1980s, the authorities initiated experiments in which enterprises were allowed to issue shares. These shareholding arrangements are described in Box 2.

Rural Land Tenure

Even more than with enterprise ownership, the formal ownership of land has changed little and re-

Box 1. China's Nonstate Industrial Sector

Over the last decade the role of the nonstate industrial sector has acquired increasing importance in the Chinese economy. Nonstate-owned enterprises have been growing rapidly, and in 1992, they accounted for a larger share of the gross value of industrial output (GVIO) than did state-owned enterprises (SOEs).

The definition of the nonstate-owned sector in the Chinese context needs to be clarified. The contours of the private sector, as commonly understood in market-based economies, are not as clear-cut in China. There are six tiers of government: central, provincial, prefecture or municipal, county or district, township, and village. Enterprises that are under the direct authority of the central government or of provincial governments are considered state owned, and all others are considered to comprise the nonstate sector. In China's official statistics, there are three main categories of nonstate enterprises: collectives, individual businesses, and "other enterprises."

Collectives can be urban or rural, depending on their affiliation. Enterprises affiliated with a district government under a municipality or a county are regarded as large urban collectives. Those affiliated with a neighborhood are labeled small collectives. In addition, urban cooperatives are included in the category of urban collectives. Rural collectives include township and village enterprises (TVEs) and rural cooperatives. What distinguishes collectives from state-owned enterprises is that they are not managed by, nor do they report to, the industrial ministries/bureaus or any representatives thereof. They operate largely in a market-based environment. From the point of view of ownership, collectives are regarded as publicly owned, because in principle their ownership is shared by the community. However, many are in effect private enterprises, because they are merely partnerships hiring several employees from the local community—which is particularly true of cooperatives. The line dividing collectives from private enterprises is thus becoming increasingly blurred.

The remaining categories of the nonstate sector together comprise what is officially regarded as the private sector. An individual business is defined as one that is owned by a household or an individual and employs no more than seven people. The category of "other enterprises" consists of private enterprises owned by a household or an individual and employing more than seven workers; foreign enterprises; and joint ventures.

The principal factors accounting for the dynamism of the nonstate sector are

- Much of the growth of the nonstate-owned sector has been in the light and service industries. These industries were severely neglected in China's industrialization strategy, which focused primarily on the development of heavy industry. Thus, one explanation for the rapid rise of collective and private enterprises was their ability to exploit successfully gaps in China's

industrial structure and respond to substantial unsatisfied demand in sectors previously repressed.
- The degree of administrative centralization in China has been much less marked than in other former centrally planned economies. Each layer of government functions as a semiautonomous operating unit and controls its enterprises along functional lines. Local governments have thus had a strong incentive to set up their own sources of finance and to keep the resources so generated within their own administrative jurisdiction. The reforms of the last decade and a half have exploited and further accentuated the decentralized nature of administration in China, which has had profound implications for the development of the nonstate sector.
- The weak bargaining position of lower levels of government has meant that, unlike the central and provincial or city level counterparts, they have been unable to provide their affiliated enterprises with the cushion of a soft budget constraint. As a result, nonstate enterprises, unlike the SOEs, have had to operate through the discipline of hard budget constraints. It is not surprising, therefore, that the nonstate enterprises have emerged as the more efficient.

If the current trends continue, the nonstate sector would account for over two-thirds of China's total GVIO, and 30–40 percent of the country's GDP by the year 2000. Such an expansion of the nonstate sector is likely to have important consequences for the entire economy, and for SOEs in particular, for which competitive pressures will rise substantially. This competition in turn is likely to constitute the single most important impetus to the reform of the SOE sector.

In assessing the future of the nonstate sector, several points should be borne in mind. First, despite considerable progress, uncertainties have persisted regarding individual ownership rights and the legal position of various forms of nonstate ownership. Second, action to improve market competition is needed. Interprovincial and even interlocality trade barriers and transport bottlenecks hamper market integration. Third, nonstate-owned enterprises have so far done well in penetrating export markets, a feat accomplished in large part through activity in processing and in partnership with the marketing skills of counterparts in Hong Kong. For the most part, they have been constrained to use foreign trade corporations as intermediaries and have not enjoyed direct trading rights. This institutional constraint lessens the ability of Chinese enterprises to learn, and it has also served to restrict the access of nonstate enterprises to foreign trade credit. Finally, a constraint that bears heavily on all industrial enterprises, and especially on those in the nonstate sector, relates to inadequate physical infrastructure. This problem will require immediate attention if the momentum behind China's nonstate sector is not to be undermined.

Box 2. Shareholding Arrangements in China's State-Owned Enterprises

Since the mid-1980s, SOEs, on an experimental basis, have begun to transform themselves into shareholding companies. These are defined as enterprises with "legal person" status that raise capital through the issue of shares. Those that issue shares to the general public are known as "joint-stock" companies. The financial liability of the shareholders is limited to the value of their shareholdings in the company. Joint-stock companies can list their shares on one of the two stock exchanges in Shanghai and Shenzhen. For others, the shares are not listed publicly but are sold through securities companies, brokerage houses, or simply to the employees of the enterprises.

The emergence of joint-stock companies and equity markets—although still of limited significance from an economic standpoint—represents a major change in the ideological framework of reforms in China: they are no longer seen as being at odds with the institutional underpinnings of a "socialist" economy. To understand the apparent paradox between the issuance of shares and the continued characterization of the ownership structure as "public," it is necessary to define the concept of "ownership." It can be defined as the right to (1) determine how enterprise assets are used; (2) receive the surplus produced by the enterprise; and (3) sell, trade, or transfer enterprise assets. This characterization of the concept of ownership in the Chinese context is attributable to the World Bank (1988). For SOEs that have been turned into shareholding companies, it is not solely the state that exercises these rights, but all shareholders, including individuals and other state and nonstate entities. In this way, shareholding is seen as being compatible with social or public ownership of the enterprises. Clearly, the potential for contradictions and conflicting objectives exists in this system. The continued preference of the authorities to maintain the predominance of public ownership presumably reflects their conviction that such a system is more equitable. However, with shareholding arrangements, ownership may become concentrated in the hands of a few individuals, thus contravening this basic objective of "social" ownership.

At first, the shares of the companies listed on the stock exchanges were issued only to domestic residents ("A" shares). Since 1991, however, some companies have been permitted to issue "B" shares, denominated in local currency, but purchased by foreigners with payment in foreign exchange. The foreign exchange is converted using the swap market exchange rate, and foreign investors are guaranteed convertibility of their investment and earnings into foreign exchange at the swap market rate. These stock markets have grown rapidly during the past two years, and the number of companies listed has risen from 15 to 60. In addition, plans are under consideration to list stocks of some companies on stock exchanges abroad. Indeed, one former SOE was listed on the New York Stock Exchange in 1992, and in 1993 some 9 enterprises have listed their stocks on the Hong Kong Stock Exchange.

The authorities see the main advantages from adopting the shareholding system as facilitating (1) the separation of government ownership from management; (2) the mobilization and rational allocation of financial resources; and (3) the provision of greater financial and decision making autonomy so that enterprises can become more efficient and respond dynamically to changing market opportunities.

With regard to the extent of state participation in shareholding companies, four levels of government ownership are envisaged. In certain priority sectors, defined as those characterized by market failures or that produced goods deemed to be of national strategic importance, enterprises will remain wholly owned by the Government. The second level will consist of enterprises with majority government ownership. The third level will comprise enterprises with minority shareholding by the Government. Finally, some small enterprises engaged primarily in commercial activities will be auctioned or leased to individuals, with the state not being represented in the ownership structure.

After an enterprise has been turned into a shareholding company, the state's position as the sole owner will disappear. As one among many owners of equity rights, the state will only participate in the decision making to the extent of its representation. The authorities envisage that, even in enterprises in which the state is the majority shareholder, the effective separation of ownership from management will be achieved by requiring that the Government act according to the statutes of the new company law that is being drafted and is expected to be promulgated during the course of 1993. Problems arising from conflicts of interest between the state as a shareholder and as the collector of tax revenues are not expected as long as the state behaves in accordance with both company law and tax laws.

In addition, state agencies will be responsible for approving the applications of state-owned enterprises to restructure themselves as shareholding companies, reviewing and approving the valuation of their assets (which would be conducted by independent appraisers), reviewing the pricing of shares, determining which state agency will actually hold the "state's" shares, and so on.

Several problems remain to be resolved with respect to these experiments. The first concerns the establishment of a strong legal framework governing the issuance and trading of shares. Second, asset valuation and accounting practices need to be standardized across enterprises. Third, the pace of reform of the social security system needs to be quickened to enable fundamental restructuring of the SOE sector. Fourth, financial sector reforms need to be accelerated so that, inter alia, banks can no longer be prevailed upon by central and local authorities to grant loans to uncreditworthy enterprises, which, in turn, has important implications for "hardening" enterprise budget constraints. Finally, some question remains on whether a true separation of the state's role as an owner and as a manager can be achieved as long as the majority or even the largest minority of shareholders are agents of the state.

mains almost exclusively under some form of public ownership. However, a fundamental change occurred in land management systems. From 1949 through 1977, collectivization of land management prevailed under a three-level system in which households were organized into production teams, which in turn were organized into brigades and ultimately into communes of, on average, 4,000–5,000 households. Private plots were tolerated on a limited scale. Under this system, land was collectively owned, and the basic production unit was the team (of, say, 20–30 households).

Three key features of the reforms of 1978 are noteworthy: first, collective ownership was retained as a fundamental precept; second, arable land was distributed among farm households based on family size and the availability of labor; and third, production decisions became the responsibility of the household governed by contracts with the relevant rural collective economic organization. Although the old system of communes, brigades, and production teams was abolished, these entities were reconstituted as townships or villages, the government of which was charged with the responsibility for land management and the negotiation of contracts with the households.

The slowdown in agricultural growth in the mid-1980s gave rise to the view that the reforms might have induced too much fragmentation of land holding and the loss of the economies of scale that

had been available under the former system. This concern has induced some adaptation of the system in the past three–five years, originating at the local level—apparently without any initiative from the center—which has led to the emergence of two types of plot in each village: one type is allocated equally to each household in the village for its private use; the other is allocated to households under contracts that are open for bidding.

In addition, shareholding cooperative systems have emerged in various parts of the country on an experimental basis by which property under the direct control of the collective is valued and divided into equal shares. Some shares are reserved for collective ownership and the rest are distributed among the village households. These shares cannot be traded but earn dividends. The administrative powers of the cooperative are vested in a board of directors, elected through a system in which each member has one vote, irrespective of the number of shares held, and decisions are made by majority vote. As a result of these experiments, farmers no longer cultivate small pieces of land but give their contracted land to the cooperative in return for shares upon which they earn dividends. The cooperative may cultivate the land or use it as a factory site, hiring labor from the households involved in the cooperative arrangement. This approach has helped solve some of the problems associated with small, fragmented land holdings.

III   Reform of the Domestic Economy

From 1978 to 1992, the Chinese leadership adopted a series of market-oriented reforms to reinvigorate the domestic economy. Although the reforms initiated were wide-ranging, they did not follow any systematic blueprint. Most were pragmatic in nature and were aimed at improving the functioning of the system or at correcting a deficiency in it. The incremental and problem-solving approach to reforms was quite successful in invigorating the economy while avoiding severe shocks to the economy. Nevertheless, there were recurring episodes of macroeconomic instability as macroeconomic management was weakened by the unevenness and incompleteness of the reforms. As a result, the authorities frequently resorted to administrative measures to restore macroeconomic balance. In late 1992, the Chinese leadership decided to break with the old planning system and to establish a fully market-based economy. This historic decision has led the leadership to formulate a comprehensive strategy to achieve this goal.

Major Reforms During 1978 to Early 1992

The reform of the domestic economy in the period through 1992 may be divided into several phases. From 1978 to 1984, reforms were aimed primarily at revitalizing the rural economy, particularly the agriculture sector. The objective was not to overhaul the planning system but to improve the functioning of the economy through the judicious use of material incentives, the encouragement of private and local initiatives, and the application of market signals to improve the allocation and distribution of resources. Many of the reform measures harked back to the policies adopted to rehabilitate the economy in the early 1960s in the aftermath of the Great Leap Forward.[16] The overwhelming success of the rural reform emboldened the leadership to adopt a wide-ranging set of measures to reform the urban industrial sector in the mid-1980s. However, because of their greater complexity, the urban reforms encountered persistent difficulties, and in 1988, the reform

efforts came to a halt when attempts to accelerate the pace of price reform led to social unrest. A period of retrenchment and consolidation followed from 1989 to 1991, during which reform initiatives were few except in the area of price adjustments and the establishment of markets for various commodities. A synopsis of the major reforms undertaken during 1978 to 1992 appears in Appendix I.

Agriculture

Until 1979, agricultural production was organized under communes that were further divided into brigades and production teams, the latter being the basic unit of production. Production decisions were passed down from higher authorities and often did not take local conditions into account. Worker remuneration was based mainly on the income of the brigade and did not reflect individual productivity, although households were allowed small private plots on which they could produce goods for their own consumption or for sale at rural trade fairs. Under this system, agricultural growth in the pre-reform era was barely sufficient to keep up with population growth.

Under the reform initiated in 1979, procurement prices of agricultural products were raised significantly, private plots were enlarged, diversification and specialization of agricultural production was encouraged, and restrictions on rural markets and non-agricultural activities were relaxed. Experiments with various forms of incentives to individuals or households eventually led to the emergence of the household responsibility system (HRS) as the dominant arrangement by the end of 1982. Under this system, plots of collectively owned land were made available to households for a fixed period under contracts that obliged the household to supply a share of the production team's mandatory production quota, to pay agricultural taxes, and to contribute to collective services.[17] The household could dispose of the remaining output on the free market or by selling it to the state at negotiated prices.

---

[16] For more details, see Riskin (1987).

[17] In 1984, the initial contract period of five years was extended to 15 years for annual crops and to 50 years for tree crops. The transfer of land use rights was legalized in 1988 to encourage private farm investment.

The reforms were highly successful in raising agricultural production, which grew at more than twice the rate of the 1960s and 1970s. However, the success was achieved at the price of increasing fiscal subsidies because the authorities were unwilling to pass the higher procurement prices to the urban consumers. The subsidies reached a peak in 1984 because of a bumper harvest, and in 1985 the state switched from the mandatory purchase quota system to a procurement contract system to alleviate the fiscal burden.

The adoption of the procurement contract system, however, led to an immediate drop in grain production as farmers diversified into more lucrative cash crops. Furthermore, infrastructure investment had declined with the breakup of the communes, which used to mobilize labor for such projects. During the next several years, the state stepped up its investment in the agricultural sector, and procurement prices offered by state agencies were raised in the late 1980s and early 1990s. As a result, grain output rose to a new peak in 1990, prompting the introduction of a market price support mechanism because the market price of grain had fallen below the state procurement price and threatened farm incomes.

As noted above, one important cost of the agricultural reforms was the sharp rise in fiscal subsidies because of the lack of price pass-through from the farmers to the urban consumers. Eventually, in 1991 and again in 1992, large percentage increases in the ration prices of these goods were implemented for the first time in about 25 years, bringing the urban sales price up to the procurement price, but still leaving subsidies on distribution and processing costs. In 1992, grain prices were decontrolled in Guangdong and Fujian provinces, and by May 1993, grain prices had been decontrolled in about 2,000 cities and counties covering 80 percent of the country.

In the last three to four years, considerable attention has been focused on developing agricultural wholesale markets as a means of reducing the role of the state in agricultural production and procurement, and gradual progress is being made in developing forward and futures trading. In May 1990, a national trading center in grains was established in Zhengzhou, Henan Province. The center makes use of contract transfers and open buying and selling. Following this, rice markets were established in Jiujiang, Jiangxi Province, and Wuhu, Anhui Province. It is estimated that there were about 72,000 open local markets throughout the country in 1992.

Rural Enterprises

One of the most important outcomes of the agricultural reform was the unexpected boom in township and village enterprises (TVEs). As restrictions affecting nonagricultural activities were progressively rolled back, rural enterprises sprang up absorbing surplus rural labor and contributing to rising foreign exchange earnings. From the start, TVEs were allowed to retain profits and achieved significant productivity gains through reinvested earnings. In addition, they were initially given concessional tax treatment, supplemented by access to credit from the rural credit cooperatives. One notable departure from the past was the freedom granted to TVEs to sell their products at market prices. Another was the change in the wage system. Previously, wages were paid to production teams and were then distributed to individual members of the team. The newly established TVEs shifted to more direct and performance-based wage payments, which greatly improved individual incentives and productivity.

The key to the early success of the TVEs lay not in any change in ownership—they remain mostly owned by the collectives—but in the extent to which market forces were allowed to sculpt their development. First, the supervising government agency had every incentive to ensure the success of the enterprise, since it was a source of revenue. Second, the TVEs faced a hard budget constraint; the townships did not have the resources to support failing enterprises, the banks would similarly be disinclined to extend credit in the absence of government financing, and unlike SOEs, TVEs have no "captive" markets for their products or inputs. Indeed, during the initial period of the rectification program in 1988–91, bank credit to TVEs was largely suspended, and many of them closed causing considerable loss of employment. Third, they were not obliged to provide social support services to the same extent as were state enterprises, were able to employ according to need, and could determine their own wage levels.

The rapid growth of the TVEs has led to a dramatic change in the economic landscape, particularly in the countryside, where they were estimated to total about 19 million and to employ more than 100 million workers in 1992 out of a total rural labor force of about 430 million.[18] It is estimated that they contributed to about half of rural GDP and accounted for about one-third of farm incomes. The gross value of industrial output of TVEs was estimated to be about one-third of the country's total in 1992.

---

[18]Another 30 million are reportedly employed by individual and small private businesses. By comparison, employment in the urban state-owned (including the government) and collective units are estimated to be about the same.

Prices and Mandatory Planning

Since most prices were controlled by the state with only infrequent changes until 1979, domestic prices did not reflect either relative scarcities or prices on international markets. In general, prices of agricultural products and basic consumer goods were kept low to protect welfare. Relative prices were structured to concentrate profits in industries producing finished products to extract fiscal revenue to support the budget. Relative prices had little effect on the allocation of resources as industrial products and raw materials were allocated by mandatory planning. Price reform has consisted of adjustments to administered prices as well as partial liberalization.

The first steps of this price reform involved substantial adjustments to agricultural procurement prices and were followed by increases in the prices of many nonstaple food items, although the prices of grain and edible oil sold under ration were not changed until 1991. The next major stage in the transition toward a more liberal pricing structure was the development of the two-track pricing system. First introduced in the rural areas, under this system farmers would sell their products (especially grain) up to the quota amount to the state at the state-fixed price, and could then sell the above-quota amount on the open market or to the state at negotiated prices. For several years the system was largely confined to agriculture and a few enterprises on an experimental basis.

In 1984, this two-track pricing was extended to cover a widening range of commodities, and over time the proportion of goods subject to mandatory planning was gradually reduced. By 1988, 53 percent by value of retail sales was transacted at market prices,[19] 28 percent took place at fixed prices, and the remainder was subject to "state guidance." Progress on price reform subsequently slowed under the rectification program, which initially witnessed a recentralization of price control.

The prices of industrial materials have also been partially liberalized, although to a lesser extent than consumer goods at the retail level. The two-track system contributed to increased efficiency by providing clearer signals for production decisions at the margin than plan prices. However, these gains were offset first by the incentives for enterprises to negotiate high levels of inputs and low levels of output, and second, by the scope for corruption that the system offers. Such persistent distortions led the authorities to decide to phase out the two-track system, and as a first step, the prices of several industrial raw materials were unified in 1991, as the authorities took advantage of the excess supply condition that had led market prices to fall close to or below the state price. No timetable has yet been set for the complete abolition of the system, but in September 1992 the authorities announced the liberalization of the prices of a large number of industrial inputs representing over four-fifths of all such commodities previously under control. For the remainder, the role of mandatory planning could be expected to be eroded by the continuation of two processes: increases in the prices of goods allocated under the plan,[20] and reductions in the proportions of goods allocated in this way.

As implementation of price guidelines has generally been left to provincial governments,[21] the intensity of price control varies across regions of the country; for instance, some provinces had decontrolled many nonstaple food prices by 1988. The authorities are also shifting away from direct price controls into "indirect" price management through the use of buffer stocks of certain basic commodities at the provincial level. First used for grain, this device was extended to other foodstuffs and some raw materials in an effort to contain inflation to targeted levels. A further consequence of devolving price-setting powers to local governments—rather than to the market—has been the emergence of market fragmentation, with a tendency for interprovincial barriers to develop against the movement of goods that remain subject to mandatory planning.

State-Owned Enterprises

Until reforms were initiated, the SOEs had little autonomy. Their production, pricing, and investment decisions were subject to the planning process, they transferred all surplus funds to the state budget, and they relied on the budget for subsidies to cover losses and grants for investment. Few incentives were available to workers or management; wages were set by centrally determined scales, and the managers' main responsibility was to fulfill production quotas.

Early reforms aimed to increase enterprise auton-

---

[19]Market prices are not entirely free of official intervention, since there are three further groups of commodities. There is a small group of perhaps 20–30 items for which producers are obliged to report their intention to increase prices. A second group consists of items for which there is strong seasonal demand, and periodically price caps are imposed. Other commodities are free of official intervention.

---

[20]For instance, in 1990, petroleum, coal, and gas prices were adjusted by 20, 45, and 65 percent, respectively, although they remained far below international levels.

[21]With the exception of the rectification program, when many controls were recentralized.

omy and accountability. After some initial experimentation, in 1983 it was decided to introduce a variant of the responsibility system that had evolved in the rural areas. Automatic profit transfers to the budget were phased out in favor of direct taxation, and from 1986 the Government reduced the extent of day-to-day intervention through the introduction of contracts for large and medium-sized enterprises.[22] Under this contract responsibility system (CRS), targets were specified for the enterprise over a three- or four-year period for its performance, its production quota to the state, and financial obligations to the Government—ordinarily taxes and dividends. Although this may have had a positive impact on enterprise efficiency, it also undermined the tax system, since the notional rate of corporate tax (55 percent) was rarely applied; instead most enterprise income took the form of contractual obligations. Moreover, to soften the impact of the increased borrowing for financing enterprise investment, loan amortization (as well as finance charges) was made tax deductible. The first generation of these contracts, signed by at least 90 percent of the enterprises, was in place by 1988.

To accompany these changes, a bankruptcy law was enacted in 1986 and became effective in 1988, but until recently it was hardly used against state-owned enterprises. In 1988 the authorities also enacted an Enterprise Law, which seeks to transform the SOEs into fully autonomous legal entities that are responsible for their own profits and losses. Detailed regulations giving effect to the broad provisions of the law were issued in July 1992.

Although the initial impact of the reforms was a recovery in the output of the SOEs, price controls persisted, production quotas for sale to the state remained part of the contracts, the SOEs had access to certain amounts of cheap raw materials, credit was readily available for investment or working capital, the budget continued to provide support for loss-making enterprises, and little advantage was taken of reforms to wage and employment practices. In short, the SOEs continued to face a soft budget constraint. In addition, they faced an uneven competitive environment in that marginal tax rates varied substantially, costs differed according to each enterprise's access to raw materials at state-fixed prices, and sales receipts depended on the proportion of output that could be sold on the free market.

The incompleteness of the reforms jeopardized macroeconomic management, with SOEs contribut-

ing to the rapid rate of credit expansion in the late 1980s and early 1990s, reflecting mounting demands on the state budget to cover enterprise losses, low revenue buoyancy, the accumulation of large inventories of unmarketable goods (either because of excess production or low quality), and the associated growth of interenterprise arrears. To address these problems, the authorities during 1991 announced some 20 measures, 12 of which were to improve the operations and external environment of the SOEs, and the others were aimed at facilitating the operation of market forces on the SOEs. Some measures, such as reducing mandatory planning, were further steps toward a market economy, but others, such as preferential access to credit and tax concessions, continued existing interventionist policies. Indeed, during the rectification program of 1988 and 1989, a large number of SOEs were given preferential access to credit and raw materials under a "mutual pledge" or "double-guarantee" system, which obliged them to deliver specified amounts of their output to the state.

Experiments were started in the late 1980s with new forms of contracting that would separate taxes from profit, end the deduction of loan amortization, and establish a lower uniform tax rate (33 percent as opposed to 55 percent). Under the new generation of contracts in 1990–91, the authorities chose to retain the existing form of contracting, although it was found that many enterprises were unwilling to undertake commitments for more than one or two years because of their financial difficulties.

Employment, Social Benefits, and Housing

Under the traditional employment system, the state assigned workers to enterprises that were obliged to provide jobs. The workers were guaranteed lifetime employment and were provided with housing, medical and retirement benefits, and a basic salary that depended on the worker's years of service. Such a system is highly rigid and resulted in overstaffing in most enterprises, with virtually no labor mobility and little correspondence between the remuneration of workers and their productivity. Hence, to make the enterprises financially accountable and to judge them by strictly economic criteria, it was necessary to change the old system of employment, social benefits, and housing so that enterprises were not burdened with social responsibilities. In the second half of the 1980s, the authorities began experimenting with reforms in these areas; however, progress was relatively slow, thus hindering reform of the enterprise system.

The labor contract system was first introduced in 1986 for all newly recruited workers in the state-

---

[22]At the same time, it introduced various forms of leasing arrangements for smaller enterprises, and to a very limited degree, the incorporation of joint-stock companies.

owned enterprises.[23] On the expiration of the contract, both the enterprise and the employee are free to choose whether to continue or terminate the contract. Under this system, the terms and conditions of employment are determined by a contract signed between the employee and the enterprise. However, progress in introducing the system was slow, and as of the end of 1992, it was estimated that the system covered only about 16 million workers or about 21 percent of the total number of employees in the SOEs.

To enforce a hard budget constraint on enterprises without adverse social consequences, an adequate social safety net has to be developed. An unemployment insurance scheme was set up in 1986 to provide benefits to the unemployed. To be eligible, the unemployment must have resulted from the following causes: (1) bankruptcy of the enterprises; (2) restructuring of the enterprises; (3) termination of labor contract; or (4) firing because of violation of rules.[24] In addition to cash relief, the unemployment scheme also provides training to the unemployed and assistance in setting up their own businesses. At present the unemployment insurance covers more than 70 million employees in the state-owned enterprises. In some regions, it extends to employees in collective firms, joint ventures, and private enterprises.

Traditionally, housing is an integral part of the employment system and is distributed to workers at a highly subsidized rate on an administrative basis. Such a system discourages the mobility of labor because the worker will generally not be able to keep his apartment if he leaves his work unit. This means that he will only move if the new employer is able to provide similar housing. This is a major constraint on labor mobility and the establishment of a labor market.[25]

Experiments with housing reform have been under way for several years in Yantai, Bengbo, Shenzhen, and Shanghai. In 1991, the pace of housing reform was speeded up with the announcement by most municipalities of major increases in rents. According to a recent household expenditure survey, the level of rent is equivalent to only 1 percent of the average household expenditure compared with 20–30 in most developed countries. The rent reform aims to increase rents over a five-year period so that the level of the rent will be equivalent to about 6 percent of household expenditure and sufficient to cover the following five cost elements: maintenance, administrative cost, depreciation, interest charges, and return on capital.

Fiscal Reform

In the pre-reform era, fiscal policy had almost no role in macroeconomic management, its function being largely confined to facilitating the administrative allocation of resources. It achieved this by regulating the rate of capital accumulation and by aiming to keep household incomes in line with the availability of consumer goods. Tax policy was not of great consequence since there were no individual or enterprise income taxes; instead, enterprises were obliged to remit all profits to the state.

The most far-reaching reforms in the fiscal area came during the mid-1980s in the area of enterprise taxation as described above. As noted by Blejer and Szapary (1989), the contract responsibility system introduced for the state enterprises implied that (1) the marginal tax rate varied widely among enterprises (declining as above-target profit rose); (2) the average tax rate faced by enterprises declined over time as inflation was underestimated in the first generation of contracts; (3) as a result, the long-term income elasticity of enterprise tax fell below unity; and (4) a strong discretionary element was introduced as enterprises sought to negotiate more favorable tax contracts. The current arrangements can be regarded as a transitional stage en route to a fully transparent tax system. Although there has been little further reform of the system since 1988, experiments with alternative arrangements have taken place.

In one major step of simplification, the taxation of all foreign enterprises and joint ventures was brought onto an equal footing in 1991, and the intention is eventually to unify the taxation of all foreign-funded and domestic enterprises. In other areas of taxation, the Government is presently reforming the tax administration system, the income tax for domestic enterprises, the personal income tax, and the value-added tax.

The adjustments in 1991 and 1992 in the prices of grain and edible oil—which accounted for the major part of food subsidies—will have a significant budgetary impact. However, a large subsidy element will remain until the retail price is adjusted to cover all costs, including processing and distribution. Similarly, the adjustments in energy prices have led to a reduction in government subsidies to loss-

---

[23]Employment reform in China is often characterized as breaking the three irons, namely, the iron rice bowl (guaranteed employment, housing, and other benefits), the iron chair (job security), and the iron wage (wages that are not related to performance).

[24]It is estimated that over 400,000 workers have benefited from unemployment relief.

[25]In the past, this lack of a housing market was a major deterrent to potential migrants into any city. However, the situation has improved in recent years as farmers in the outskirts of the cities have constructed houses for rent to rural migrants.

making enterprises. However, further adjustments are necessary before the fiscal subsidies can be completely eliminated.

Resource sharing between the center and provincial governments has received considerable attention. One objective is to preserve an adequate degree of fiscal control for the central government and another is for the center to have more resources at its disposal to implement the priorities of the central government, including transfers to provinces in deficit. The contracts signed with the provinces in 1988 implicitly contained a pro-cyclical bias, such that expenditures were likely to increase when revenue earnings in the provinces were high.[26] Although a new generation of contracts should have become effective in 1991, thus far the existing contracts have been extended. Meanwhile, in 1992, the authorities experimented with a system of separate taxation in nine provinces and municipalities with the aim of delineating more clearly the taxes that accrue to the central government or to the provinces and those that are shared.

Financial Sector

Banking System

Until 1978, the banking system had only a limited role, acting as the means of providing the credit needed by the enterprises to implement the physical plan. As enterprises acquired greater responsibility for implementing their own investment programs (with diminishing access to budgetary funds), greater scope opened up for involvement by the banking system. However, for the first few years of the reform period, there was little change from a banking system in which the People's Bank of China acted as a monobank, functioning as both central bank and commercial bank. At the same time there were three other specialized banks whose activities were sharply demarcated into agriculture, state construction, and foreign exchange management.

In 1984, the People's Bank was established as a central bank, and its commercial banking functions were transferred to a newly created bank. At the same time, the specialized banks were gradually allowed to engage in general banking activities including, from 1986, foreign transactions. Thus, although considerable specialization remained, the basis for a competitive environment began to be laid

as new banks at the provincial level and two comprehensive banks were set up.

After the major reforms of the mid-1980s, the pace of reform in the financial sector slowed appreciably from 1988 under the rectification program. Considerable recentralization took place, the role of directed credit became more important, and there was some loss of competition within the banking sector with more uniformity in interest rates and a sharpening of the demarcation lines between the specialized banks. In late 1990 and 1991, some of the rigidities were eased: the restrictions on lending to nonpriority sectors were relaxed (allowing TVEs renewed access to credit), and provincial branches of the People's Bank were allowed some discretion in allocating credit among banks.[27] There is also a growing interbank market that operates largely at the municipal and provincial levels.[28] Nevertheless, the central bank still played an important role in intermediating funds between surplus and deficit provinces and between branches of banks.

Nonbank Financial Institutions

The nonbank sector has grown considerably throughout most of the period since 1978. Trust and investment companies (TICs), whose activities include domestic currency loans, direct investment, and trust business (in which the TIC acts as an intermediary in lending between two enterprises), expanded rapidly after the mid-1980s. So rapid was this growth that the Government temporarily restricted their operations to investigate their financial condition. With a few exceptions, they were judged to be in sound financial condition and their operations were soon normalized. This episode illustrates the inadequate development of the supervision of financial institutions (including banks). Other financial institutions have been established, engaged in leasing, insurance, and securities transactions, and some finance companies were formed by enterprise groups to handle a range of financial services for these groups.

International trust and investment corporations have operated since 1979, including a number at the provincial level, particularly in the coastal regions. Their function is largely to raise funds from foreign sources to finance foreign-funded enterprises through loans and equity participation; they have been the primary source for most international bond issues made by China during the 1980s.

---

[26]Although there are a number of variants, the typical contract between the province and the center is similar to that with the enterprises in the sense that revenue transfers are contracted according to revenue in a base year with annual increments agreed upon ex ante.

[27]About 5 percent of the total credit quotas of specialized banks are set aside for the provincial branches of the People's Bank to allocate at their discretion.

[28]Most of the transactions are between branches of specialized banks and are arranged through a financial intermediary sponsored by the local branch of the People's Bank.

Securities Markets

The first issues of securities in 1981 were exclusively treasury bonds sold involuntarily to enterprises and individuals. In the case of bonds for individuals, the yields were set slightly higher than the interest rates on bank deposits of comparable maturity. The Government later began to issue bonds whose proceeds were earmarked for key investment projects. Experiments with the issuance of enterprise "shares" began in 1982 for private enterprises and in 1985 for state enterprises.[29]

The development of a secondary market in government securities has been encouraged by the authorities since 1988, and in 1990, it was enhanced by the establishment in Beijing of a national electronic trading system (STAQ) that links several cities across the country. The development of the treasury bond market was given a boost in 1991 when the Ministry of Finance switched from the administrative placement of bonds to marketing the bonds through underwriting by financial institutions.

In 1990–91, securities exchanges were opened in Shanghai and Shenzhen, which permitted trading in government and enterprise bonds, as well as shares of joint-stock companies. Initially, only Chinese residents were allowed to trade in the enterprise shares. However, in early 1992, foreigners were allowed access to these exchanges to procure and trade in special issues of enterprise shares ("B" shares). Attempts by local governments to open more securities exchanges in 1992 have been resisted by the central authorities, which are concerned about the lack of experience and expertise in operating such exchanges. In late 1992, the central authorities set up two regulatory bodies to oversee and supervise the development of the securities industry. In addition, a national securities law has been drafted and is under consideration by the legislative agencies.

Monetary Policy Instruments

Prior to the reforms, monetary policy was implemented through a credit plan—the financial counterpart of the physical plan specifying output targets—and a cash plan, which took into account various factors affecting the demand for currency. Because of the fixity of prices, the demand for money (currency) was highly correlated with cash incomes. An excess supply of money had little impact on prices or the balance of payments and manifested itself in the form of an involuntary increase in savings deposits.

The changing institutional structure of the finan-

cial system and the gradual increase in the openness of the economic system have enhanced the importance of monetary policy in demand management. The principal instruments of monetary policy include direct controls on credit and interest rates, and indirect instruments, notably reserve requirements and lending to banks by the People's Bank. However, since indirect instruments of monetary policy have yet to be fully developed and deployed, the credit plan continues to be the principal instrument of monetary policy. Changes in interest rates and in reserve requirements are of secondary importance.

Extending the Reform Agenda: 1992 and Beyond

A new phase in the reform and opening up the Chinese economy began in 1992 with a marked acceleration in the pace of reform. The process was initiated early in the year during Deng Xiaoping's trip to south China in which he made some important pronouncements and called on the country to accelerate its growth and pursue more vigorously its policy of reform and opening up. It culminated in October at the Fourteeth National Congress of the Communist Party of China, when the party endorsed the views that he had expounded and called for the establishment of a "socialist market economy." In March 1993, the goal of establishing a socialist market economy was enshrined in the country's constitution during the first session of the Eighth National People's Congress.

This section discusses the plans and strategies proposed by the authorities to broaden and deepen the reform process to transform the economy into a fully market-based economy. Unlike the previous section, the discussion here is thematic, proceeding from the most general and abstract to the particular and specific. It first reviews the plans to strengthen the legal and regulatory framework and to reform the role and functions of government and the macroeconomic framework. It then proceeds to discuss the initiatives announced to establish markets and deepen reforms in specific sectors of the economy. Box 3 contains a chronology of reforms implemented since early 1992.

Legal and Regulatory Framework

The legal and regulatory framework is one of the weakest areas in China's economy today. Unlike a central planning system that operates mainly on administrative decrees and directives, a market system requires an elaborate legal and regulatory framework to set the "rules of the game" within which market participants can operate competitively and freely. Many new laws and regulations have to be

---

[29]These shares did not convey any right of ownership but paid interest and a dividend.

drafted and older ones annulled, amended, or revised in several areas of the economy to reflect the new requirements of a market economy. In addition, the legislature has to be strengthened to create the necessary institutions to monitor and supervise the markets and to establish an impartial judiciary to arbitrate disputes. The challenge in this area is to effect a clear separation between the different institutions of the state on the one hand and to define as precisely as possible the rights and obligations of the various participants in a market economy on the other.

In 1992, the authorities announced that the work on drafting legislation was to be speeded up. During the past year and a half, several important economic laws have been enacted. These include a patent law, a copyright law, a tax administration law, the Import and Export Commodities Inspection Law, and a trademark law. The State Council also promulgated several important regulations to give effect to laws that had been passed previously. These included the Regulations on Changing the Operating Mechanism of Enterprises, Regulations on the Formation of Shareholding Companies, a code for the implementation of a new accounting system for enterprises, and the Interim Provisions on the Management of the Issuing and Trading of Stocks. Other important economic legislation being drafted or revised comprise a central bank law, a general banking law, a securities law, an insurance law, enterprise and personal income tax laws, a contract law, a real estate law, and a company law. In June 1992, the central government delegated to the Shenzhen municipal government the legislative power to formulate and enact new laws to promote economic reforms with the aim of speeding up the legislative work in the country.

On the regulatory side, the State Council set up a Securities Exchange Commission and a Securities Supervision and Administration Commission in 1992. Other institutional measures to be implemented include the adoption of a new accounting framework that is more suited to a market system, the reform of bank supervision, the establishment of public auditing firms, and the formation of law firms to provide legal services to the business sector. A new accounting system for enterprises was implemented beginning on July 1, 1993, which is of special importance because it will provide a more accurate picture of the performance of enterprises. The accounts of the enterprises will also be subject to audit by public auditing firms instead of the supervising ministries.

Role and Functions of Government

An important aspect of economic restructuring is to redefine the role and functions of government in the economy. In particular, the government should withdraw from its traditional tight control of enterprises. It should instead focus on establishing an effective macroeconomic management system; developing and improving the economic infrastructure to enable markets to operate efficiently; establishing and improving the social security system; and providing services to economic agents. It is also essential to change the parochial attitude of the local governments to break down the internal barriers to trade and to movements in labor and capital and encourage the establishment of national markets.

In 1992, the authorities announced that a major restructuring of the administrative system would be implemented over the next three years to make the role and functions of the Government conform to the requirements of a socialist market economy. In general, those ministries and agencies that were in charge of mandatory planning and the supervision of enterprises would be either restructured, merged, or abolished. In March 1993, the National People's Congress approved a plan to streamline the government bureaucracy. The number of ministries and departments under the State Council was reduced from 86 to 59. As a complement, the civil service is to be restructured, with the number of staff reduced by one-third and the remainder subject to major redeployment to make their work relevant to the needs of a market economy. The State Planning Commission is being revamped to shift the focus of its work away from the traditional task of physical planning toward macroeconomic planning and the development of long-term economic plans.

Macroeconomic Management

The reform of the system of macroeconomic management is recognized as a key task of the Government during the coming years. Since 1978, China has experienced at least three major episodes of macroeconomic instability during which emphasis on deepening reforms was subordinated to the restoration of macroeconomic stability through economic and administrative means. Hence, a key objective of macroeconomic policy is to maintain a stable environment for the pursuance of reform and the opening-up policy.

Although the system of macroeconomic management has been reformed since the mid-1980s to incorporate elements of indirect instruments, it still relies to a large extent on administrative methods and instruments. Such a system is incompatible with the principle that the behavior of economic agents should be guided by market forces. The authorities have begun to implement a plan to restructure the Government to reduce the role of physical planning in the economy and the direct supervision of enter-

Box 3. Chronology of Reform Initiatives, 1992–July 1993

1992

January	Senior leader Deng Xiaoping visited south China and called for acceleration of growth and reform and the opening up process.
January 1	Tariffs on 225 import items reduced.
January 11	Announcement that wholesale market in sugar to be opened in Tianjin and Guangzhou.
March 10	Waigaoqiao Free Trade Zone in Shanghai began to operate. Announcement that similar zones to be opened in Tianjin, Shenzhen, Dalian, Guangzhou, and Yangpu during 1992.
March 11	Announcement that civil service system to be established by 1995.
March 17	State Council approved more preferential policies for Shanghai, including autonomy to approve access of domestic enterprises and joint ventures to the Waigaoqiao Free Trade Zone; to approve project with value below Y 200 million; to issue Pudong construction bonds of Y 500 million each year; and to issue $100 million of "B" shares each year.
March 18	"Provisions of Import and Export Tariff of the People's Republic of China" introduced to be made effective April 1.
March 20	Meeting of National People's Congress (NPC). Announcement of formal termination of the rectification period and adoption of 1992 budget.
April 1	Import adjustment tax abolished. Prices of rice, corn, and flour increased by Y 0.22 a kilogram or about 44 percent; as compensation, monthly income of workers was raised by Y 5.
May 8	Announcement that foreign banks to be allowed to open more branches in Guangzhou, Dalian, and Tianjin, and the SEZs.
May 11	"Provisional Measures Concerning Registration of Owners of the State-Owned Assets" issued jointly by the State Assets Management Bureau, Ministry of Finance, and the State Industrial and Commercial Bureau.
May 23	Ministry of Finance and State Commission for Restructuring the Economic System (SCRES) jointly issue new accounting system for shareholding enterprises.
May 28	Shanghai Metals Exchange opened.
June 9	State Council announced opening of 28 inland cities to foreign trade and investment. Cities to be granted the same preferential policies as the 14 open coastal cities.
June 10	State Council announced opening up of 14 cities on the border with neighboring countries to foreign trade and investment.
June 17	Set of codes and regulations for adopting a joint stock company published.
June 20	Experimentation with system of separate taxation between central and local governments conducted in nine provinces and municipalities.
June 20	Standing Committee of National People's Congress calls for speeding up the drafting of legislation on company law, act on bills of exchange, securities law, planning law, banking law, and so on.
June 24	Ministry of Finance issued new accounting system for foreign-funded enterprises.
June 28	Retail sector opened to overseas retailers.
July 2	Shenzhen given power to enact legislation.
July 4	System of securities management working conference with representatives from ten ministries set up under the State Council with Governor Li Guixian as chairman.
July 10	Announcement that Chinese accounting system to be reformed. "Guidelines of Basic Accounting Principles" to be issued soon.
July 13	"Provisional Wage Regulations for Shareholding Enterprises" issued jointly by Ministry of Labor and SCRES.
July 21	Announcement that Bank of China to be floating foreign currency bonds in the domestic market.
July 23	"Regulations on Transforming the Operating Mechanism of State-Owned Enterprises" issued by the State Council Economic and Trade Office.
July 23	Premier Li Peng reported that economy grew by 10.6 percent in first half and revised growth target for the 1990s to 9–10 percent.
July 24	People's Bank of China appointed seven accounting firms in Hong Kong to audit accounts of 35 enterprises that have applied for listing in Shenzhen and Shanghai.
July 30	Finance Minister Wang Bingqian announced fiscal reforms: separation of taxes between central and local governments; separation of profit from taxes of enterprises; a two-tier budget system; reform of tax system; introduction of new accounting system; and reform of state asset management system.
August 4	Capital Steel Corporation granted approval to set up its own bank (Huaxia Bank).
August 6	Ministry of Communications announced opening up of transportation to foreign investors.
August 7	Press report that 66 industrial enterprises declared bankrupt in the first half of the year.
August 8	The National Foreign Exchange Adjustment Center opened in Beijing. The center is fully computerized and consists of dealers from 42 local swap centers across the country.
August 11	"Provisional Regulations of Land Property Management of Enterprises" promulgated by the State Land Management Bureau and the SCRES.

August 13	Ministry of Commerce decided to build international vegetable market in Shandong province.
August 23–29	Hainan government granted a Japanese firm (Kumagai Gumi) the right to use and develop 30 square kilometers of land in the Yangpu Economic Development Zone. The price for the land use rights—HK$18 billion ($2.3 billion)—was the highest ever paid by foreign investors.
September 2	State Price Administration announced lifting of price control on 570 types of production materials.
October 10	Memorandum of understanding signed with the United States that committed China to significant liberalization of its trade regime over next few years.
October 10	Import substitution list on 1,700 items eliminated.
October 12–21	Fourteenth National Congress of the Communist Party endorsed the views of senior leader Deng Xiaoping and adopted goal of establishing a "socialist market economy." Growth target for the 1990s set at 8–9 percent a year.
October 20	Announcement that implementation of new enterprise income tax to be accelerated from three years to one year.
October 28	State Council set up the National Securities Committee under Vice Premier Zhu Rongji to formulate laws and regulations in the securities market; the Securities Supervision and Administration Committee to supervise and regulate the securities industry.
November 17	"Detailed Measures on Changing the Business Mechanism of State-Owned Commercial Enterprises" promulgated, which aims at making state-owned commercial enterprises autonomous and competitive.
December	Price controls on meat, eggs, and vegetables lifted.
December 31	Tariffs on 3,371 import items reduced by an average of 7.3 percentage points.

1993

February	People's Bank of China issued 16 provisions to regulate activities in interbank markets.
Late February	Standing Committee of NPC approved country "Product Quality Law" to come into effect on September 1, 1993.
March	Chinese residents allowed to take Y 6,000 abroad.
Early March	Cap imposed on swap market rates.
March	First session of Eighth National People's Congress. Election of new government to a five-year term. Constitution amended to eliminate reference to a planned economy and to enshrine the goal of establishing a "socialist market economy."
March 31	Establishment of Beijing Financing Center to take over from former Beijing Financial Market.
April 14	Regulations on transactions in foreign exchange swap markets.
Mid-April	State Council issued circular calling for halt to unauthorized bond issuance.
April	State Council approved two regulations to improve safety nets for job waiting and laid-off workers: "Regulations on the Unemployment Insurance" and "Regulations on Arrangement of Redundant Workers of State-Owned Enterprises."
April	Eight enterprise groups selected to experiment in state assets management.
April	State Administration for Exchange Control decided to allow trading of foreign currencies by local individuals in Guangzhou and Shenzhen.
Late April	State Council approved "Provisional Regulations on the Management of Stock Issuance and Trade."
Late April	State Administration of Industry and Commerce announced issuance of "Provisional Regulations on the Registration and Management of Futures Market."
April 28	National Electronic Trading System (NETS) put into operation: a national electronic computer system for trading of stocks and bonds. It relies on satellite communication to link the major cities.
May 7	Chinese press (Capital Economic Information) announced that the Chinese Government had decided to establish a development bank to undertake long-term policy lending.
May 10	Grain coupons abolished, and price controls on soy sauce, vinegar, and milk lifted in Beijing. Workers compensated with a Y 10 a month cash subsidy. It was reported that grain coupons had been eliminated in 1,800 cities and counties in 27 provinces and autonomous regions accounting for 80 percent of the country's total cities and counties.
May 15	Interest rates raised averaging 1.8 percentage points for term deposits and 0.8 percentage points for working capital loans. Interest rate from 11 percent to 14.06 percent a year for five-year treasury bonds and from 10 percent to 12.52 percent for three-year treasury bonds.
Mid-May	State Council issued circular imposing strict control on establishment of special development zones.
May 27	Shanghai Petroleum Exchange opened for trading.
June 1	Administrative cap on swap market rate abolished.
July 1	New accounting system implemented.
July	People's Bank introduced 16 point program to re-establish control over financial system, including increases in interest rates.

prises by government ministries. The intention is to rely mainly on indirect instruments to manage the economy. However, indirect instruments of monetary and fiscal policy are effective only if enterprises are faced with a hard budget constraint and banks behave competitively and are sensitive to their cost of funds. The reform of the macroeconomic management system implies therefore not only the development of new instruments of monetary and fiscal policy but the successful restructuring of the enterprises and the financial institutions.

In the monetary area, the People's Bank has announced its intention to move away from the credit plan toward greater reliance on indirect instruments of monetary policy, including open market operations, interest rates, reserve requirements, and relending to banks. To prepare for the eventual use of open market operations, the authorities are taking steps to develop the instruments and the interbank markets. A modern payments system is being established that will enable the banks to manage their funds more efficiently. This will in turn enable the People's Bank to influence monetary conditions by affecting the liquidity of the banking system.

To strengthen the role of the budget in macroeconomic management, the authorities are taking steps to correct the structural weakness in the fiscal system, particularly the lack of revenue buoyancy, the erosion in the central government's share of fiscal revenue, and the high subsidy payments. Over the years, the budget has been weakened by a progressive narrowing in the tax base, which is highly dependent on the state-owned enterprises, and the adoption of the contract responsibility system.[30] To broaden the tax base and improve the elasticity of the tax system, a new enterprise income tax is to be introduced that will subject all domestic enterprises to a uniform tax rate of 33 percent and require the payment of amortization and dividends from after-tax profits.[31] Other tax reforms under consideration include the introduction of a new personal income tax, the reform of indirect taxes, and the strengthening of tax administration. To strengthen the central government's control over fiscal revenue, the current revenue-sharing contracts with the provinces

will be replaced by the establishment of separate taxation for the local and central governments. On the expenditure side, the high subsidy payments are expected to diminish over time as controlled prices, particularly of coal and grain, are adjusted further. On a more analytical aspect, the authorities are also reforming budgetary procedures and adopting a new budget format that is more suited to macroeconomic analysis.

Establishment of Markets and Related Infrastructure

A major task during the coming years will be to establish the environment and facilities for developing national markets in all types of commodities and services. Since 1978, local markets have developed spontaneously as a result of the liberalization in the agricultural and industrial sectors. For instance, free markets in food and consumer goods can be found in all urban areas. However, the development of national and regional markets has been hampered by the inadequate legal and regulatory framework, poor economic infrastructure, particularly transportation, telecommunications, and the payments system, and the protectionist tendency of local authorities.

In recent years, the authorities have actively organized and established wholesale markets at the regional and national level, such as the garment market in Shengyang; the clothings market in Suzhou; the meat market in Chengdu; the sugar market in Guangzhou; and the vegetable and grain market in Shandong province. National and regional trading centers have been established for various commodities and services. These include the national grain trading center established in Zhengzhou in 1990; the nonferrous metals exchange in Shenzhen (1992) and the metals exchange in Shanghai (May 1992); the securities exchanges in Shanghai (December 1990) and Shenzhen (May 1991); the petroleum market in Nanjing and Shanghai; the cereals and edible oils market in Shanghai; and the national foreign exchange trading center in Beijing.

In general, the authorities are involved in providing the facilities and setting up the legal and regulatory framework to ensure that the markets work efficiently and fairly. Policies were adopted in 1992 to promote the development of the service sector, which is essential to the smooth functioning of markets. In particular, a market economy requires the professional services of accountants, auditors, property valuation experts, lawyers, management consultants, marketing agents, commercial artists, and so forth. To overcome the infrastructure problem, the authorities are undertaking major investments in transportation and telecommunications. A modern payments system is also being established.

---

[30]Under the old central planning system, the SOEs played a key role in extracting surplus from the economy for investment and for financing the budget. With the rapid growth of the nonstate sector, the tax base of the budget has shrunk because the nonstate sector is subject to lower taxes or tax exemptions. For an elaboration of this point, see McKinnon (1992).

[31]Enterprises with incomes below a certain level are subject to a lower rate of 24 percent, whereas enterprises located in the special economic zones will continue to pay a special rate of 15 percent.

Table 6. Proportion of Output and Sales at Fixed, Guided, and Market Prices
(In percent)

	1978	1987	1990	1991	1992
Agricultural output					
Fixed prices	92.6	29.4	25.0	22.2	17.0
Guided prices	1.8	16.8	23.4	20.0	57.8
Market prices	5.6	53.8	51.6	57.8	68.0
Industrial output					
Fixed prices	97.0	...	44.6	36.0	20.0
Guided prices	—	...	19.0	18.3	15.0
Market prices	3.0	...	36.4	45.7	65.0
Retail sales					
Fixed prices	97.0	33.7	29.7	20.9	10.0
Guided prices	—	28.0	17.2	10.3	10.0
Market prices	3.0	38.3	53.1	68.8	80.0

Sources: *China Price Yearbook*, 1990; and data provided by the Chinese authorities.

Price Reform

The Chinese authorities have made considerable progress in the area of price reform. Since 1984 when the authorities introduced a dual-track pricing system, China has succeeded in transforming its price system from one in which most prices are set by the state to one in which they are determined by a combination of administrative and market forces. Nevertheless, the price system has remained complex, and the dual-track pricing system tends to encourage corruption and rent-seeking behavior by enterprises. Also, the subsidies to consumers and enterprises have become a heavy burden on the budget. The authorities have recognized that the completion of price reform will greatly facilitate reforms in other areas of the economy, particularly enterprise and fiscal reforms.

In 1992, the authorities announced a speeding up in the pace of price reform. In particular, the time frame for the elimination of the two-track pricing system would be compressed to the next three–five years instead of over the decade. Major adjustments were made to the price of many commodities including grain, flour, coal, steel, cement, gas, and transportation services. Furthermore, in the wake of an acceleration in the pace of enterprise reform, the number of producer goods subject to mandatory price control was reduced from 737 to 89. The authorities also reduced the share of output of coal and other products subject to mandatory planning. As a result, the proportion of producer goods subject to price control was reduced to 20 percent and that of consumer goods to 10 percent in 1992 (Table 6). At present, only seven types of agricultural products, including grain, cotton, and tobacco, still fall under state control. As noted above, by May 1993, controls on grain prices had been lifted in about 2,000 cities and counties covering about 80 percent of the country.

Agriculture

Of all the major reforms introduced since 1978, perhaps the most successful and complete is the change in the organization of agriculture. Since 1983, the household responsibility system has remained the principal organizational form of farming. This system has now been written into the country's laws to assure the farmers that it will not be changed arbitrarily. As in recent years, future reforms will focus on the distribution and pricing system through the establishment of national and regional wholesale markets and the realignment and liberalization of prices. By 1992, a three-tier system of national trading centers, regional wholesale markets, and local open markets had been established throughout the country. With regard to the pricing system, it was reported that about 70 percent of all agricultural products were set by the market at the end of 1992 and only 17 percent continued to be subject to prices fixed by the state. By mid-1993, controls on grain and other food prices had been lifted in most parts of the country.

Enterprise Reform

Perhaps the most difficult task ahead is the successful transformation of the state-owned enterprises (SOEs) into autonomous, competitive, legal entities that are responsible for their own finances. As described above, experiments with enterprise reform have been under way since 1983, and SOEs now enjoy much greater autonomy than in the past. However, the autonomy is not complete as enterprises are still subject to administrative interference from their supervising ministries, and, furthermore, the greater autonomy has not been accompanied by a corresponding hardening of the budget constraint. The weakness of the state enterprise sector was demonstrated vividly during the last macroeconomic cycle (1988–91), when the financial difficulties of the SOEs forced the authorities to relax the stance of monetary and fiscal policy to resuscitate the economy. Even in 1992 when the economy was experiencing robust growth, it was reported that about one-third of the SOEs were making losses that put a strain on the financial system. Hence, one of the priorities of the authorities is to speed up enterprise reform with the aim of pushing the SOEs into the markets and making them autonomous and responsible for their profits and losses.

Enterprise Regulations

To make enterprises truly autonomous, the authorities need to sever the link between the SOEs and their supervising ministries. In July 1992, the authorities published the "Regulations on Transforming the Operating Mechanism of State-Owned Enterprises." These regulations are intended to give effect to the "Enterprise Law," which was enacted in 1988 to harden the budget constraint of state-owned enterprises by transforming them into autonomous legal entities responsible for their own profits and losses. The regulations spell out 14 decision-making rights that enterprises should enjoy, including the right to decide what to produce and how to price and market their products, how to invest their funds, the right to hire and fire workers and to decide on wage policy (see Box 4). In return for these rights, enterprises are expected to be accountable for their performance, and inefficient ones are expected to restructure or to be closed in accordance with the bankruptcy law. The role of the state as owner of the enterprises is delegated to the State Asset Management Bureau. The new regulations have been promulgated and are in the process of being implemented by the various government departments and provincial authorities. However, according to recent reports, implementation of the regulations has been resisted.

Shareholding System

An important experiment in enterprise reform that has major ramifications for the ownership structure of enterprises and that has received widespread in-

---

Box 4. Enterprise Regulations

Enterprises shall enjoy the following rights:
- To make production and business decisions;
- To set their own prices;
- To market their own products;
- To purchase materials;
- To import and export;
- To make investment decisions;
- To decide on use of retained earnings;
- To dispose of assets in accordance with production requirements;
- To form partnerships and mergers;
- To assign labor;
- To have personnel management;
- To set wages and bonuses;
- To determine internal organization;
- To refuse arbitrary levies and charges.

---

terest is the shareholding system. Under this system, enterprises are allowed to restructure themselves into limited liability companies by issuing shares. The shareholding system (or corporatization) provides for a clear separation between the ownership and management of the enterprises and is therefore a way of restructuring the traditional relationship between the Government and the enterprises under its control. It is estimated that several thousand enterprises are participating in this experiment. Because of the great interest in the shareholding system, the authorities have issued several codes and regulations on the formation of such enterprises, including the system of management and accounts. A company law has been drafted and is under consideration by the legislative authorities.[32]

The development of the shareholding system has been boosted by the establishment of stock exchanges in Shanghai and Shenzhen to list the shares of approved joint-stock companies.[33] The stock markets have grown dramatically in the last two years, with the number of shares listed rising from 15 to 113 (of which 21 are "B" shares) by mid-1993

---

[32]The authorities do not regard the conversion of state-owned enterprises into shareholding companies as "privatization," which has the connotation of wholesale conversion of state-owned enterprises into private enterprises. Instead, they see this as a means of raising funds for restructuring and of introducing a more effective management system while retaining a significant ownership share and ultimate control over the companies.

[33]These are shareholding companies that issue shares to the general public and that may apply for listing on the two stock exchanges. In the restructuring, the proportion of the share belonging to the state, municipality, or township is determined by an appraisal company according to the net value of the asset in the enterprise accruing to the state, municipality, or township.

and the combined capitalization was estimated at about Y 100 billion in 1992. Two regulatory agencies were set up to oversee the development of the industry in 1992. In April 1993, a national electronic trading system (NETS) was established in Beijing to allow trading in legal persons shares. A new securities law is being drafted to unify the rules and regulations in the country. At present, the two securities exchanges are operating under their own separate rules and regulations.

In the view of the authorities, the shareholding system can be an effective vehicle for restructuring enterprises. Except for large enterprises in strategic sectors of the economy such as defense and high technology, most SOEs could eventually be converted into shareholding companies with the state retaining a majority or significant share. This would allow the state to exercise effective control over the companies while permitting the enterprises to adopt modern management practices and to raise funds, in both local and foreign currencies, for restructuring and growth. In 1992, a large state-owned enterprise was converted into a shareholding company and listed on the New York Stock Exchange. Plans are under way to list the stocks of nine other companies on the Hong Kong Stock Exchange.

Enterprise Groups

Another experiment that is being encouraged is the formation of large enterprise groups with the aim of rationalizing the industrial structure by taking advantage of economies of scale and promoting the optimum use of resources. Unlike many former centrally planned economies, China's economy is highly cellular, as each locality was encouraged to be fully self-reliant during the pre-reform period. Furthermore, enterprises within one branch of an industry were normally not allowed to diversify into related fields. As a result, from a national perspective, there is much duplication, a lack of specialization, and strong local barriers to interregional trade. The aim of the authorities is to break down the departmental, regional, and ownership barriers in the economy and create large conglomerates that are efficient and competitive internationally. In the past two years, the Government has selected 55 large enterprise groups (out of an estimated 1,600 such groups) for restructuring to strengthen the role of the parent or core enterprise within each group, particularly its management of the subsidiary enterprises. Preferential treatment such as trading rights or the right to diversify into other fields of activity are being provided to these 55 enterprise groups to encourage their development into competitive conglomerates.

Loss-Making Enterprises

The authorities are taking special measures to deal with the loss-making enterprises according to the nature of their losses and the current low level of development of the social safety net. It is estimated that about 70 percent of the losses of state-owned enterprises are policy induced, mainly because of price control.[34] If these enterprises are to be financially independent, it is necessary to liberalize the prices of the goods and services they produce. As noted above, price controls were lifted on 593 types of production materials in September 1992. It is intended to liberalize the prices of coal and other energy products over the next three–five years to avoid major disruption to the rest of the economy. In the interim, the losses of those enterprises will continue to be subsidized through the budget.

For the remaining enterprises that are experiencing losses because of poor management, the authorities are providing fiscal and financial incentives for them to restructure or move into other lines of production. Several thousands of the smaller enterprises have been either closed or merged with more profitable ones to rationalize their operations. In the commercial sector, many state-owned stores have been leased out to private individuals. In some cities, experiments are being carried out to allow foreign investors to buy into and restructure existing loss-making state-owned enterprises.[35] Finally, the authorities are cautiously applying the bankruptcy law to the enterprises; it was reported that 66 enterprises were declared bankrupt in the first half of 1992.[36]

Surplus Labor and Tertiary Sector Development

The problem of surplus labor is one of the most difficult issues in reforming the enterprise system. It is estimated that the redundancy in the government

---

[34]These enterprises are mainly concentrated in the transportation and energy sectors.

[35]In late 1992, a Hong Kong investor paid $3 million to buy a 51 percent share in a state-owned textile factory in Wuhan. The factory was converted into a shareholding company, a new management was introduced, and more than half of the work force of 2,230 was retrenched. Also, a major company was recently established in Hong Kong that has bought into state-owned enterprises in several coastal cities with the aim of restructuring them into profitable enterprises. In Sichuan province, it was reported that 16 small to medium-sized SOEs would be auctioned off to foreign investors in 1993.

[36]Although the bankruptcy law was enacted in 1986, it was rarely applied in the early years because of strong resistance from the workers and the commitment of the authorities to guaranteed employment. However, in 1992–93, the law has been applied more frequently as the unemployment insurance scheme has developed and the attitude of the public has changed.

and state-owned enterprises may be as high as 20 million workers out of a total work force of 104 million.[37] To avoid massive unemployment, the authorities are encouraging the development of the tertiary sector to absorb the surplus labor. Under the old planning system, tertiary activities were considered unproductive and were therefore not encouraged; as a result, many of the services that are essential to the smooth functioning of a market system were neglected. Since the onset of the reform process, the tertiary sector has grown from about 21 percent to 27 percent of GNP, but it is still small in comparison with the average of 60 percent in most developed countries. In July 1992, the authorities announced several policies to stimulate the development of this sector, including encouraging the use of foreign capital and know-how; transforming most tertiary businesses into profit-oriented enterprises; encouraging staff in government organizations and SOEs to resign and establish businesses in the service sector; decontrolling the prices of most products and services; and providing financial and tax incentives.[38] The authorities view the tertiary sector as having great potential for absorbing surplus labor because this sector is generally more labor intensive, comprising, for instance, retailing and wholesaling, catering, teaching, consulting, and social services. It is envisaged that the tertiary sector will play a role similar to that played by the township and village enterprises in absorbing the surplus labor in the agricultural sector during the 1980s.

Employment, Social Security, and Housing

To speed up enterprise reform, the authorities have recognized that they will also need to accelerate the reform of employment, social security, and housing. In 1992, they announced that reform of the employment system would be accelerated. A modified version of the labor contract system is being encouraged for adoption by all enterprises as soon as possible.[39] Under this modified system, all employees, including managers, technicians, and operators, must sign a contract with their enterprises to decide their duties, rights, and benefits. The maturity of the contracts can either be fixed or open ended. Under this system, certain distinctions among employees such as permanent versus contract

and cadres versus workers will be abolished. A professional grading system will be introduced and all employees will be recruited through examinations. As a complement to the labor contract system, a labor arbitration system is being developed to mediate in labor disputes. To replace the system of job assignment by the state, employment agencies are being established to help place the new entrants in the labor force.

To extend the social safety net, the authorities are formulating new regulations and plans to improve the benefits and expand the coverage of the unemployment insurance system in the near future. In particular, unemployment benefits will be provided to all involuntary unemployment regardless of cause, and the coverage will be extended to employees in collectively owned and foreign enterprises. Further, to facilitate enterprise restructuring, some of the funds will be used both to provide training for the surplus labor in the SOEs and to develop new jobs.

In the past, retirement benefits were provided by enterprises out of current revenue. In recent years, retirement funds have been set up whereby workers and employers are required to contribute a certain percentage of the payroll toward the funds.[40] At present, such funds are established at the municipal level in most cities and counties and at the provincial level in about 12 provinces. The intention is to establish a unified national retirement fund at an appropriate time in the future. The retirement funds have improved the conditions for labor mobility and have relieved enterprises of the burden of providing for their retired workers.

To encourage the development of a housing market, the authorities have announced a program of rent adjustment aimed at reducing the subsidy element in housing. This development should lead to the commercialization of the housing sector. Encouragement of the sale of housing is another component of the housing reform. In the last few years, many real estate companies have been established that contract apartments for sale at market prices. However, most of the sales are to overseas residents (for example, residents of Hong Kong). The sale of housing to domestic residents is made difficult by the low wages (reflecting the payment of subsidies in kind) and the general lack of housing finance. To overcome this problem, some municipal authorities have set up housing funds—to be funded from the issuance of savings bonds and the sale of existing housing—to construct low-cost housing and expand

---

[37]In the rural sector, it is estimated that redundancy may be as high as one-fourth of an estimated labor force of 430 million.

[38]These policies are described in the Decision on Expediting the Development of the Tertiary Industry published on July 16, 1992.

[39]In Shanghai, it was reported that 976 SOEs employing 1.34 million workers or 78 percent of the city work force had adopted the labor contract system by end-1992.

[40]These funds are modeled on the Central Provident Fund of Singapore. In Shanghai, the contributions by both the employers and the employees are set at 5 percent of the wage bill.

the housing stock. In some cities, financial institutions are being established aimed at developing mortgage financing. A major source of funds for such institutions is the savings from retirement funds that are being established across the country.

Land Use System

Reform of the land use system is a major element in the overall strategy to establish a market economy. In the past, land was allocated free of charge to users on an administrative basis. Since 1987, when the land use right for a piece of state-owned land in Shenzhen was auctioned to a foreign investor, a lively real estate market has developed. The Government has enacted several laws in the last few years to regulate the real estate industry.[41] Under the land administration law, since all land belongs to either the state or the collectives, the state is encouraged to implement a system of land use rights based on the leasehold system. Such land use rights are transferable, and enterprises (domestic and foreign) that acquire the land use rights are allowed to develop, use, and administer the land. The maximum term for the use of land is 70 years for housing, 50 years for industrial purposes, and 40 years for commercial purposes.

So far most of the sale of land use rights for industrial purposes has been by public bidding or negotiated agreements; however, in the past year, the authorities have been encouraging the auction of land use rights, particularly for commercial and residential development. By September 1992, it was estimated that about 3,100 plots of land with a total area of 13,500 hectares had been transferred. The revenue from the sale of land use rights (estimated at Y 50 billion in 1992) accrues mainly to the local governments and is likely to become a major source of funds for urban renewal because most of the land use rights in the cities are still under the state.[42] In Shanghai, for instance, it was reported that the municipal authorities collected Y 2.7 billion from the

sale of land use rights in 1992. About 85 percent of the revenue is retained by development companies to be used for infrastructure development and the rest is used to compensate the original occupants of the land.

Financial Reforms

China's financial system has become more diversified since 1984 with the emergence of many new financial institutions providing a variety of instruments and services to customers. Notwithstanding all these changes, the state banks have continued to be regarded essentially as administrative organs of the state responsible for mobilizing and providing funds to finance important activities of the public sector, including those of the state-owned enterprises. As a result, the specialized banks were obliged to provide policy-based loans that were not based on commercial criteria.[43] Furthermore, because of the decentralized structure of the banking system, the banks were susceptible to local political pressure to provide loans for investment projects and to give credits to loss-making enterprises to keep them afloat.

In late 1992, the authorities announced plans to reform the banking system to transform the specialized banks into competitive, autonomous, and self-accountable commercial entities. Regulations to apply the Enterprise Law to the banking system are being drawn up. The main components of the reforms are (1) separating commercial from policy-based lending; (2) separating quasi-fiscal from commercial operations so that all loans will be provided at market interest rates and any interest subsidies will be provided through the budget; (3) funding long-term loans for investment projects from long-term funds; and (4) encouraging banks to improve their loan assessment and portfolio management. A new accounting system consistent with international standards is being implemented, and the supervision system of the People's Bank over the banking system will be reformed to focus on banks' prudential management of risk.[44] Key aspects of the banking reforms are expected to be incorporated in the banking laws that are being drafted.

Another element of banking reform is the establishment of a modern payments system and the development of a national interbank money market

---

[41]The main laws include (1) the Law on Land Administration enacted in June 1986 and amended in December 1988; (2) Provisional Regulations Concerning Sale and Use of State-Owned Land in Cities and Towns; and (3) Regulations for Implementation of the Land Administration Law promulgated by the State Council in February 1991. The Law on Land Administration states that all land belongs to either the state or the collectives, all land should be registered and recorded by local governments, which shall issue certificates for land use rights, the land use rights are transferable, and a leasehold system of land use rights shall be implemented.

[42]For transfers of land use rights in the secondary market, a progressive tax is imposed on the appreciation in their value. To prevent speculative transactions, transfers of land use rights are allowed only after 25 percent of the original investment has been fulfilled.

---

[43]The three main categories of policy-based lending are financing of state investment projects, credits for grain procurements, and trade credits for mandatory imports.

[44]An important issue to be dealt with is the restructuring of the balance sheets of the specialized banks to separate out nonperforming loans that arose from policy-based lending in support of government policies, including those of local governments.

that will allow the People's Bank to conduct open market operations. At present, the interbank market is fragmented into numerous locally based markets organized through financial intermediaries sponsored by the local branches of the People's Bank. Also, because of the decentralized structure of the banks, the interbank market consists mainly of borrowings between branches of banks. Most banks rely on the People's Bank for refinancing and only turn to the interbank market as a last resort, which in part reflects the distortion in interest rates. Because of the weakness in the regulatory framework, the interbank market, which grew rapidly in 1992, has been marked by many irregularities in lending practices. In early 1993, the People's Bank introduced new regulations to strengthen supervision over the interbank market. One objective of the interbank market reform is to encourage banks to reduce their reliance on the People's Bank for refinancing and to centralize and improve their management of funds. The People's Bank is also planning to allow greater flexibility for interest rates, and it has introduced short-term bills that can be used as instruments for open market operations.

In the nonbank financial sector, the authorities are promoting the establishment of institutions to provide medium- and long-term funding for investment purposes. As noted above, the equity capital market is developing rapidly with the spread of the shareholding system and the establishment of securities exchanges in Shanghai and Shenzhen and two national electronic trading systems in Beijing. In the past year, the treasury bond market has received a setback because of a failure to adjust interest rates sufficiently in the face of rising inflation. A strong capital market will help to reduce the vulnerability of the banking system by providing enterprises with an alternative source of long-term funding; at the same time, households can invest their longer-term savings in higher yielding assets. The authorities are taking steps to strengthen the regulatory framework in this sector.

Nonstate Sector

The success of China's reform efforts thus far is attributable in large measure to the impressive growth of the nonstate sector during the past decade and a half, particularly of the township and village enterprises (see above) and the joint ventures (see Section IV). Although less conspicuous, there has also been a boom in individual and private businesses, concentrated mainly in the urban areas. It is estimated that by 1991, there were about 140,000 privately owned companies (which produced Y 100 billion worth of goods) and 15.3 million individual businesses employing 24.7 million people. In 1991, 7.72 million—89 percent—of the retail sales outlets in China belonged to private companies or individually employed businesses. The nonstate sector has contributed to the reform process not only through its strong performance but also by absorbing surplus labor and providing competition to the state enterprises. The encouragement of the nonstate sector is regarded as an integral part of the overall reform strategy.

IV Opening Up and External Policies

A key feature of the Chinese reforms was the gradual opening of the economy to the rest of the world and the concomitant change in the official attitudes to foreign trade and investment. The approach was initially conceived with the relatively modest goals of transferring technology to China and of boosting export earnings to acquire essential imports for industry, while minimizing recourse to foreign borrowing. To this end, a number of limited areas were designated as open economic zones (OEZs)[45] in which outward-oriented activity would be promoted.

The OEZs were also used as laboratories for experimenting with market-oriented reforms in a microcosm, on the original presumption that they could be isolated from the rest of the economy. However, their strong performance and growing regional autonomy in government led to pressures for greater integration with the domestic economy and they have emerged as centers of the most dynamic growth in the economy (Tables 7 and 8).

The process of opening the economy inevitably necessitated the reform of policies and institutions in the external sector. China has gradually undertaken an extensive reform of its exchange and trade systems, which nonetheless remain complex, restrictive, and lacking in transparency. Assessing the precise degree of liberalization is complicated in a system in which the implementation of policies has become highly decentralized. Although it is clear that, in principle, China's exchange and trade systems remain subject to many restrictions and distortions, China's growing integration into the global economy suggests that the actual application of external policies tends to be relatively liberal, albeit selectively so.

This section reviews the evolution of external economic policies at the national level—specifically the exchange and trade systems—and at the regional level with a focus on the development of the OEZs.

Policies at the National Level

Trade System

Until 1978, China's foreign trade was conducted through 12 state-owned foreign trade corporations (FTCs) organized along product lines. These corporations procured and traded the quantities directed by the central plan, and all profits and losses were absorbed by the state budget. In turn, production enterprises, which did not have direct access to foreign markets, were given production targets under the plan for supply to the FTCs. Through this system, the tradable goods sector was insulated from the rest of the world, and the balance of payments was controlled through the trade plan.

Under the reforms, the FTCs were progressively given greater autonomy and made more accountable for their operations, while administration of the system was decentralized to the provincial authorities, which were given authority to establish their own FTCs. By 1989, most local branches of national FTCs had become independent entities responsible to the local authorities for their financial results, bringing the number of FTCs to about 4,000. A growing number of enterprises could trade on their own account.

At the same time, the degree of mandatory planning was progressively reduced, guidance planning became more important, and, most significant, the trade conducted by foreign-funded enterprises (FFEs) rose substantially. By 1991 exports and imports subject to mandatory planning had fallen to 30 percent and 20 percent of their respective totals, while the trade of FFEs reached some 20 percent of total exports by 1992.[46] As the role of the trade plan

---

[45]The term "open economic zones" in this paper covers the many forms of areas and zones that are designed to promote foreign trade and investment in China. They include the special economic zones, open coastal cities, the delta areas, and the development zones opened in many inland and border cities since 1992.

[46]The guidance plans assign targets to provinces and FTCs for the values of exports and imports of a range of products (in some provinces the guidance was given de facto mandatory status by the local governments). In 1991, the guidance plan accounted for 15 percent and 20 percent of exports and imports, respectively.

Table 7. Basic Indicators of SEZs and Open Coastal Cities, 1991

	Special Economic Zones[1]	Open Coastal Cities	All China
Population (*in millions*)	2.2	28.4	1,143.33
Population as percent of China's total	0.2	2.5	100.00
GDP (*in billions of yuan*)	21.8	152.3	1,768.60[2]
GDP as percent of total	1.2	8.6	100.00
GDP/population (*in yuan*)	9,810	5,360	1,540
Investment in fixed assets (*in billions of yuan*)	8.3	39.5	444.93
Exports (*in billions of U.S. dollars*)[3]	8.8	32.4	62.19
Exports/GDP (*in percent*)[3]	193	101	0.17
Exports as percent of China's total	14.2	52.1	100.00
Actual foreign investment (*in millions of U.S. dollars*)	856.5	1,973.6	5,498.8
Actual foreign investment as percent of China's total	15.6	35.9	100.00
Actual foreign investment/total fixed investment	49	24	11

Source: *China Statistical Yearbook,* 1991.
[1] Excluding Hainan.
[2] Reference is to GNP.
[3] Exports from the SEZs and open cities may be overstated because of their status as entrepôts for the surrounding regions.

has declined, direct control over exports and imports has continued through a licensing system for both.[47] External trade taxes have also played an increasing role in influencing the quantity and commodity composition of trade flows, and other means have been used to influence the level of external trade, most notably import substitution regulations, which were used (on a nonmandatory basis) to limit imports of about 1,700 goods produced domestically.

Starting in 1991, a number of new measures were taken to liberalize trade, in part stimulated by China's efforts to make its trade conform with international practices in the context of its application to resume its membership in the General Agreement on Tariffs and Trade (GATT).[48] All direct budgetary export subsidies to foreign trade corporations were eliminated from January 1991, and export tariffs on mineral ores were reduced. Import duties were reduced on a number of occasions,[49] and China's customs duty regulations were replaced with the harmonized commodity description and coding system (the average level of duty rates under the new

tariff structure is generally equivalent to that under the old structure). In April 1992, the import regulatory duty—established in 1985 as an import surtax—was eliminated, and in October 1992 it was confirmed that the import substitution regulations had been terminated. In addition, under a memorandum of understanding with the United States, China announced its intention to publish the many internal regulations on foreign trade to increase the transparency of the system. Other trade-related measures included a revision of the patent law to bring it into line with international conventions and various steps toward establishing legal conventions and practices for the conduct of external trade.

Looking to the future, China has announced its intention to undertake a number of measures in the context of its negotiations to resume its participation in the GATT, and in the memorandum of understanding with the United States published on October 10, 1992. These include

(1) The removal of two-thirds of import licensing requirements by the end of 1994, and the reduction of other nontariff measures. The memorandum contains a commitment to eliminate all import restrictions, quotas, licensing requirements, and controls on a wide range of products by 1997, with about three-fourths of such restrictions eliminated within two years.

(2) Measures to promote the transparency of the trade system, including the publication of all laws, regulations, and decrees that govern trade, and to

---

[47] In 1991, licensing covered 55 percent of exports and 40 percent of imports.

[48] During 1992, lengthy negotiations with the United States culminated in a memorandum of understanding that entailed a substantial liberalization of bilateral trade.

[49] The most substantial of these was on December 31, 1992, when customs tariffs were reduced by an average of 7.3 percentage points on 3,371 items representing 53 percent of dutiable items.

Table 8. Selected Indicators of SEZs and 14 Coastal Open Cities

	Annual Industrial Growth Rate, 1984–91[1] (In percent)	Exports/GDP, 1991[2] (In percent)	Foreign Investment, 1991 (In millions of U.S. dollars)	Foreign Investment/ GDP, 1991 (In percent)
China total	12.1	16.7	10,290	2.8
Dalian	15.1	237.3	443	15.8
Qinhuangdao	15.8	212.4	6	1.0
Tianjin	8.5	86.1	481	8.9
Qingdao	9.5	161.4	62	3.0
Yantai	16.2	53.5	38	5.1
Lianyungang	10.4	101.3	11	2.5
Nantong	10.8	46.8	34	5.1
Shanghai	6.7	89.1	855	7.5
Ningbo	14.2	71.0	36	3.0
Wenzhou	14.6	21.5	6	1.4
Fuzhou	15.1	59.1	167	15.2
Guangzhou	15.7	165.6	267	4.5
Zhanjian	28.5	85.7	19	2.5
Beihai	21.1	49.9	9	5.3
14 coastal open cities	9.9	116.8	2,434	7.2
As percent of China total	82.2	701.3	24	262.1
Shenzhen	41.2	382.6	477	18.5
Zhuhai	45.4	186.3	157	13.6
Shantou	27.0	252.9	197	27.0
Xiamen	24.7	118.7	183	17.1
4 SEZs	34.2	273.5	1,013	18.3
As percent of China total	282.9	1,641.6	10	663.5

Sources: *China Statistical Yearbook*, 1992; and IMF staff estimates.
[1] The national consumer price index was used to deflate industrial output to constant prices.
[2] Trade data for the coastal cities reflect their use as entrepôts for the surrounding region.

establish a central repository for the publication of all trade regulations.

(3) Making the import approval process more transparent by identifying which agencies of the central government can issue directives, bans on imports, quotas, licensing requirements, restrictions, and controls.

Exchange System

During the early stages of reform, various arrangements were tested for sharing foreign exchange with the objective of improving incentives for exports. A retention system evolved, under which exporters surrender their actual foreign exchange and are issued retention quotas by the State Administration for Exchange Control (SAEC) equivalent to a portion of such earnings. Through 1990, a complex set of regulations had developed that allocated foreign exchange differently according to industrial type and provincial location (in general, the coastal provinces were more favored). In 1991, a signifi-

cant simplification occurred under which a uniform retention rate for enterprises was set throughout the country, and standard formulas were established for sharing foreign exchange between the center and the localities. During the 1990s, experiments with cash retention have been undertaken (notably in Hainan, Shanghai, and Shenzhen).

Until 1980, several exchange rates were used for trade transactions between the FTCs and domestic enterprises with which they were trading. In 1981, a single exchange rate was established for the internal settlement of trade transactions that remained more depreciated than the official exchange rate. Over the succeeding three years the official exchange rate was progressively devalued, and in 1984 the rates were unified.

A dual exchange rate re-emerged in 1986 with the establishment of the foreign exchange adjustment centers (FEACs or swap centers) at which approved enterprises were permitted to buy and sell retention quotas (Box 5). Initially, the system was restrictive because the exchange rate (in fact, the premium paid

Box 5. Foreign Exchange Retention and the Swap Centers

The Post-1991 Retention System

The new rules announced in February 1991 introduced more uniformity into the foreign exchange retention scheme, replacing the previous system of retention that had differentiated on the basis of commodity and location. For general commodities, exporters (other than foreign-funded enterprises, which can retain 100 percent of export earnings if located in a special economic zone) must surrender all foreign exchange earnings to the state at the official rate and receive retention quotas for 80 percent of such earnings—100 percent for mechanical and electrical products. These retention quotas are distributed to the foreign trade corporation (60 percentage points); the supplying enterprise (10 percentage points); and the local government (10 percentage points). The state also has the option to purchase 20 percentage points of the retention quota from the FTC and the 10 percentage points from the supplying enterprise at the prevailing swap market exchange rate. It appears that the state did exercise the option fully in 1991 and 1992, thereby acquiring 50 percent of export earnings for official purposes, compared with an average of 56 percent in the period before the new system.

Criteria for Access to Swap Market Purchases

Access to swap centers to purchase foreign exchange is subject to approval and is restricted mainly to enterprises that need foreign exchange either to import goods that are consistent with the industrial policy of the state or to service their foreign currency debt. Purchases of actual foreign exchange are usually limited to foreign-funded enterprises. Retention quotas may be procured at the swap centers by domestic enterprises that are certified by the Ministry of Foreign Economic Relations and Trade (MOFERT)—now known as the Ministry of Foreign Trade and Economic Cooperation (MOFTEC)—(or its regional counterpart) as eligible to import. These quotas may then be used within a six-month period to acquire foreign exchange from the state reserves at the prevailing official rate.

Authorization to purchase on the swap centers is granted by the SAEC based on two criteria. For licensed imports, if an enterprise has received MOFERT approval, the enterprise is allowed access to the swap center. For those imports that do not require a specific license, SAEC approval is based on a "priority list" of uses of foreign exchange compiled in conformity with the state industrial policy. Priority is given to such goods as fertilizers and other agricultural inputs, imports of foreign-funded enterprises, and the imports of advanced equipment by large and medium-sized state-owned enterprises. Lower priority is given to requests for foreign exchange to finance imports of consumer goods and luxury items. However, in practice, imports of such goods by foreign trade corporations using their own retained foreign exchange earnings are relatively unrestricted. Moreover, there is considerable variation in the degree with which local SAECs enforce the priority list in their regions.

Trading Procedures

An electronic open bidding system is used in 18 of the nearly 100 swap centers in the country, at which authorized dealers and brokers trade openly on a trading floor in retention quotas and U.S. dollars (also Hong Kong dollars in Shenzhen). Prices are allowed to fluctuate freely during each trading session. The People's Bank of China can intervene to smooth out the trading and to limit the fluctuations, although such interventions are rare. In most other places, the swap center is an office within the SAEC that matches written applications to supply or buy retention quotas where applicants must appear in person with the requisite documentation.

Exchange Rate Developments

After freer trading was permitted in 1988, the premium on the exchange rates in the swap centers rose to about 80 percent, reflecting an increased number of participants at the same time as aggregate demand was surging (Chart 1). In 1989, the premium fell sharply in the wake of a devaluation of the official exchange rate, and thereafter the differential between the two rates narrowed to about 8 percent. Since April 1992, the renminbi has depreciated markedly in the swap market. Despite continued small adjustments of the official rate, the spread between the official rate and the average swap rate had widened to about 45 percent by early 1993, at which point the authorities attempted to

for the retention quotas) was set by the authorities and participation was limited to foreign-funded enterprises.[50] In 1988, as experience was gained, all enterprises with foreign exchange retention quotas were granted access to the centers. At the same time, the authorities lifted control on the swap market exchange rate, allowing it to be determined through negotiations between buyers and sellers. In December 1991, all domestic residents were allowed to sell foreign exchange at the swap rate at designated branches of banks; since then, there has been virtually no restriction on the sale of foreign exchange in the swap centers. However, restrictions remain on purchases, and for about three months in early 1993, the authorities attempted to cap the swap

---

[50]One major purpose of the original arrangements was that they provided FFEs with a means to meet a prevailing exchange control requirement that they should maintain a balanced foreign exchange position.

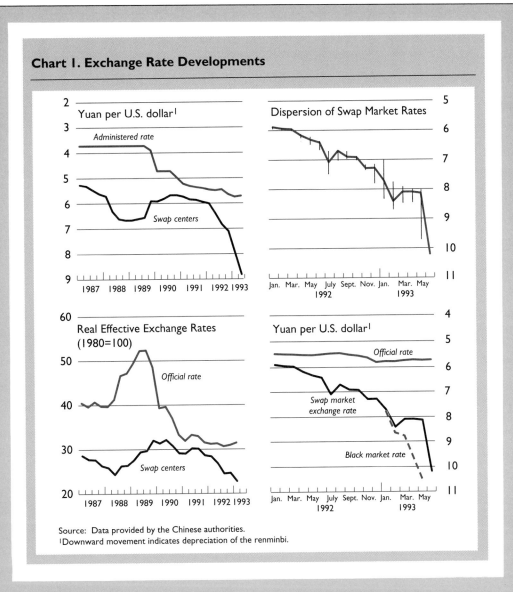

Chart 1. Exchange Rate Developments

Yuan per U.S. dollar[1]

Administered rate

Swap centers

1987 1988 1989 1990 1991 1992 1993

Dispersion of Swap Market Rates

Jan. Mar. May July Sept. Nov. Jan. Mar. May
1992 1993

Real Effective Exchange Rates
(1980=100)

Official rate

Swap centers

1987 1988 1989 1990 1991 1992 1993

Yuan per U.S. dollar[1]

Official rate

Swap market
exchange rate

Black market rate

Jan. Mar. May July Sept. Nov. Jan. Mar. May
1992 1993

Source: Data provided by the Chinese authorities.
[1]Downward movement indicates depreciation of the renminbi.

cap the premium in the market. As this merely had the effect of driving most transactions out of the swap centers into the black market, the cap was lifted in June 1993. There was an immediate step adjustment, with the premium widening to 80 percent by mid-1993, but the rate moved only gradually thereafter. This depreciation occurred against the background of strong import growth stemming from rapid economic growth, an investment boom, and trade liberalization initiatives.

market exchange rate (see Box 5). This effort was abandoned when it became evident that most transactions were being driven into the black market.

With the new exchange arrangements in 1986, the official exchange rate was in effect pegged to the U.S. dollar.[51] There were two devaluations in 1989 (21 percent) and 1990 (9 percent), and in 1991, small frequent adjustments in the official rate were made. By April 1993, the real effective exchange rate of the official exchange rate had depreciated 33 percent more than in 1986 and 70 percent more than in 1980. The authorities have indicated that the ultimate goal is unification of the exchange rates and convertibility of the currency.

[51]Since 1987, the exchange rate has been formally classified by the IMF as a more flexible arrangement (other managed float). See the IMF's *Annual Report on Exchange Arrangements and Exchange Restrictions*, various issues.

Policies at the Regional Level[52]

In the context of opening the economy, China's regional policy has centered on developing OEZs, a process that has evolved through four stages broadly in parallel with reforms in the rest of the economy (see Section III). The first stage began with the establishment of four special economic zones (SEZs) in 1979–80. The intention was to replicate the successful experiences of similar zones in some newly industrializing countries in Asia,[53] although the SEZs were more ambitious in terms of policies, activities, and geographical coverage than traditional export processing zones.[54]

During the second stage, these policies were extended to other areas when 14 coastal cities were given authority in 1984 to establish "open zones" within their jurisdictions. The third stage saw the establishment of Hainan as an SEZ in 1988 and the opening of the most ambitious of the OEZs in Shanghai—Pudong New Area in 1990. The most recent stage followed Deng Xiaoping's initiative in early 1992 that gave priority to an acceleration of economic reforms and further opening of the economy. A number of major cities in inland provinces—particularly along the Yangtze River valley—and on the borders with neighboring countries have also been authorized to offer preferential policies to foreign investors and export-oriented enterprises. See Table 7 for basic data on the SEZs and open coastal cities.

The preferential policies that have been offered to foreign-funded enterprises operating in OEZs since the early 1980s include partial exemptions and holidays from corporate income tax; duty-free imports of goods to be used as inputs for export production; full retention of foreign exchange earned through exports; and free access to foreign exchange adjustment centers (Tables 9 and 10). Although these preferential policies initially varied from zone to zone, there have been recent efforts to harmonize them. Foreign entities have also been entitled to purchase land use rights since 1990 (although these leases were not actively traded until 1992).

As regards the taxation of corporate incomes, foreign-funded enterprises operating in the OEZs generally pay, after their tax holidays expire, half of the tax rate they would be expected to pay outside

the zones. To be eligible for any of the tax exemptions and reductions, the initial investment to set up a foreign-funded enterprise must be for a contracted period of at least ten years. Other tax exemptions and reductions are available to foreign-funded enterprises in all zones if they bring advanced technology into the country, export at least 70 percent of their output, or are involved in developing infrastructure. In addition to these tax exemptions and reductions, the tax rates applied on enterprises in each zone are sometimes negotiated on an individual enterprise basis. Many domestic enterprises also operate in these zones under policies similar to, but less generous than, those offered to the foreign-funded enterprises.

Special Economic Zones[55]

The Original SEZs

The application of China's policy of economic opening to the rest of the world began with the establishment of four SEZs in the two coastal provinces of Guangdong and Fujian in 1979–80. Three of these SEZs are in the southeastern coastal area of Guangdong: Shenzhen (near Hong Kong); Zhuhai (near Macao); and Shantou. The fourth is located in Xiamen in the southeastern part of Fujian across from the Taiwan Province of China. These SEZs, which remained the only OEZs in China through 1984, had the particular advantage of easy access to foreign markets. Otherwise, they were located in regions that had relatively few innate advantages: Guangdong's level of development was average for China in the late 1970s, whereas Fujian was one of the poorest regions prior to reform.[56]

Enterprises operating in the zones include (1) state enterprises owned by local authorities or by authorities of other provinces; (2) enterprises that are wholly foreign owned; (3) equity joint ventures; and (4) contractual joint ventures.[57] Wholly owned foreign-funded enterprises in the zones generally make their own decisions with respect to their or-

---

[52]The term "regional" is used to allude to the several tiers of public ownership and administration other than the central: provincial, municipal, county, township, and village. Most references in this paper relate to policies and developments at the provincial and municipal level.

[53]Zou, Ma, and Wang (1990), p. 2.

[54]One major difference is that enterprises operating in SEZs are not obliged to export all of their output.

[55]Including the special economic zone of Hainan Island.

[56]Per capita national income in Guangdong was Y 313 in 1978, almost the country's average of Y 315, whereas in Fujian it was only Y 233, ranking it twenty-fifth among the 29 provinces.

[57]Equity joint ventures are limited liability corporations in which Chinese and foreign partners invest and operate jointly, sharing the profits, losses, and risks. Contractual joint ventures may involve the foreign partner providing technology and a capital input, but with a predetermined schedule of return negotiated in advance. The Chinese partner usually provides land, materials, the work force, basic buildings, and services, and so forth.

Table 9. Income Tax Incentives in Open Economic Zones

Region	Income Tax Rates[1, 2]	Tax Holiday/Exemption
SEZs	15 percent income tax	1980–83: Exemption for first profit-making year and 50 percent reduction for second and third years for firms with a scheduled duration of over 10 years.
		Dec. 1984– : Two years' tax holiday from the first profit-making year (for services the holiday is 1 year), followed by a 50 percent reduction in the 3 following years for firms with a contract life of 10 years or longer.
Hainan	Dec. 1988: 15 percent income tax	May 1988: Five years' tax holiday from the first profit-making year, and a 50 percent reduction in the sixth to tenth years, for firms in certain infrastructural and agricultural areas, with a contract life of 15 years or longer.
		— Same as other SEZs for projects in industry and other infrastructure.
		— Firms producing export goods (70 percent or more of total output value) or with high technology are allowed to deduct 10 percent income tax after the 3-year tax reduction.
Economic and technological development zones of 14 open coastal cities	Dec. 1984: 15 percent income tax	Dec. 1984: Same as SEZs.
Other parts of the 14 open coastal cities	General rate: 24 percent Dec. 1984: 15 percent income tax for technology-intensive investment of $30 million or above.	1984–91: 20 percent tax reduction for firms in certain fields.
		July 1991: Exemption in first two profit-making years and 3-year 50 percent reduction afterwards.
Pudong New Area	Sept. 1990: 15 percent income tax	Sept. 1990: Basic provisions are the same as SEZs (for business in services the holiday is 1 year).
		— Firms producing export goods (70 percent or more of total output value) or with high technology are allowed to deduct 10 percent income tax after the 3-year tax reduction.
		— Investment in infrastructure is offered more tax exemptions or deductions.
Inland areas	Nov. 1981: Progressive marginal rates for CJV and FOV in the range of 20–40 percent.[3]	July 1991: Exemption for first two profit-making years and 3-year 50 percent reduction thereafter. Enterprises exporting more than 70 percent of their production volume are subject to a 50 percent reduction on the income tax for the production year.

Sources: *Guide to China's Foreign Economic Relations and Trade: Cities Newly Opened to Foreign Investors; Almanac of China's Economy*, 1981, 1991; Kueh (1987); *China's Investment Guide*, 4th ed., 1989; Osborne (1986); *An Introduction to China's Coastal Open Areas*, 1991.

[1] In all open economic zones a 10 percent surcharge on profits is imposed by the local government, which has the discretion to grant exemptions.

[2] Until 1991, all open economic zones granted exemptions from a 10 percent withholding tax that was applied throughout China. This tax was abolished in July 1991.

[3] CJV: contractual joint venture; FOV: wholly foreign-owned venture; and EJV: equity joint venture.

ganizational and personnel structure, wage systems, and the recruitment or dismissal of employees. With the authorities' approval, they can sell part of their output in the domestic market.

One important difference between the SEZs and other areas in China was the administrative decentralization that permits investment decisions in the SEZs to be taken largely outside the state plan. Local authorities in SEZs are allowed to attract foreign investors[58] through preferential policies. They are also allowed to undertake their own infrastruc-

[58]Domestic investment from other areas of China has also taken place in the SEZs.

Table 10. Incentives in Open Economic Zones

Region	Import and Export Duties and Consolidated Industrial and Commercial Tax (CICT)	Other Incentives[1]
SEZs	1980–83: Exemption of import duties for production inputs. Many imported consumer goods are exempted from import duties. Dec. 1990: Unified exemption of import duties and CICT for production inputs and export goods.	Flexible entry visa service.
Hainan Special Economic Zone	May 1988: Exemption of import duties, product tax, and value-added tax for imported inputs for production. Export goods are exempt from the same tax.	Flexible entry visa service; land use rights can be transferred to foreign investor for 70 years.
Economic and technological development zones of 14 open coastal cities	Dec. 1984: Inputs for exporting production are exempt from import duties. Export goods are exempt from CICT.	
Other parts of open coastal cities	Dec. 1984: Inputs for exporting production are exempt from import duties. Export goods are exempt from CICT.	
Pudong New Area	Dec. 1990: Exemption of import duties for production inputs. Export goods are exempt from export duties and CICT.	Investment in infrastructure and banking are encouraged.
Inland areas	Dec. 1990: Inputs for export production are exempt from import duties. Export goods are subject to export duties and CICT.	1984: Rebate of 40 percent income tax if the profit is reinvested for joint ventures. July 1991: All foreign-invested enterprises get tax refund for reinvestment.

Sources: *Guide to China's Foreign Economic Relations and Trade: Cities Newly Opened to Foreign Investors; Almanac of China's Economy*, 1981, 1991; Kueh (1987); *China's Investment Guide*, 4th ed., 1989; Osborne (1986); *An Introduction to China's Coastal Open Areas*, 1991.
[1]Experiments with transfers of land use rights became more widespread in many of the open economic zones from 1992.

tural development and other investment as long as they can raise the funds from taxation, from profits of the enterprises they own wholly or partly, or from banks in the zones.[59] Enterprises in the zones have the right to make their own investment, production, and marketing decisions. This relative autonomy has been an important factor in attracting investment resources from other areas of China as well as from abroad into the SEZs.

Another important consideration is the tax incentives available to foreign investors. FFEs are subject to 15 percent tax on profits,[60] compared with 33 percent paid by those located outside the SEZs. In addition, after a tax holiday in the first two profit-making years, they pay only 7.5 percent tax during the following three years. FFEs located in the SEZs are exempt from import licenses and from customs duties on imports of machinery, equipment, and other inputs, as well as on their exports. These products, excluding cigarettes, liquor, and petroleum products, are also free of indirect taxes if sold within the zones. However, if FFEs sell imported goods that have not been further processed in the SEZs, they must pay 50 percent of the full duty and indirect taxes.[61]

The four SEZs together have recorded impressive results in terms of their exports, foreign direct investment flows, and industrial output. The value of their exports doubled from 1987 to 1991, reaching $6.6 billion, or about 9 percent of China's total.[62]

---

[59]In certain cases some financing for such investment has come from policy-based lending, supported by credit from the central bank.

[60]This was the rate applied in Hong Kong at the time the policy was formulated. It is also applied on domestic enterprises in SEZs. Elsewhere, domestic enterprises are subject to a 55 percent corporate income tax. However, in practice tax paid is based on negotiated tax contracts.

[61]Under certain conditions, goods manufactured in the SEZs can be sold in other areas of the country provided full payment of import duties and indirect taxes is made. Domestic enterprises operating in the SEZs need government approval to enjoy these advantages.

[62]However, according to the customs data (which may include exports originating in other parts of China), the value of their exports, including Hainan province, reached $9.6 billion in 1991 or 13.4 percent of China's total.

Table 11. Cross-Country Comparison of Tax Rates

	Income Taxation
China	Corporate income tax: 15 percent in SEZs and open cities; 33 percent on foreign-owned enterprises in other areas.
Hong Kong	Corporate income tax: 18.5 percent Other entities: 17 percent Taxes are levied on profits and interest arising in or derived from Hong Kong
Malaysia	Corporate income tax: 35 percent Development tax: 5 percent Excess profit tax: 3 percent
Singapore	Corporate income tax: 31 percent Withholding tax: 33 percent on dividends earned in Singapore
Korea	Corporate income tax: 0–30 percent
Thailand	Corporate income tax: 35 percent Business tax: 1.5–40 percent Remittance tax: 20 percent

Source: Grub and Lin (1991), p. 65.

Contracted foreign investment in 1991 was more than eight times its 1987 level and total real gross industrial output showed strong gains, increasing by over 35 percent in 1991.[63] Data for the first half of 1992 and other provisional reports indicate a substantial further increase in activity.

The good performance of the SEZs can be illustrated by the success of Shenzhen, the largest of the original four. Shenzhen's exports, which accounted for more than half of total exports of the four SEZs in 1987–91, increased during that period to $3.5 billion (or $5.8 billion, based on customs data). Contracted value of foreign direct investment attracted into Shenzhen increased from $274 million in 1987 to over $1 billion in 1991. Shenzhen's industrial output is estimated to have grown by 40 percent in 1992. These developments reflected the activities of some 20,000 enterprises, of which about 5,000 were foreign-funded ventures.

The success of these original SEZs may be attributed to a number of factors: (1) the incentives given to foreign investors that were more generous than those made available in other countries;[64] (2) their small initial size coupled with the fact that they were the only areas in China opened to foreign investment before 1984, which enabled them to receive very large amounts of investment; and (3) the large amount of domestic investment that came in the form of joint ventures established by provincial authorities from other coastal and inland provinces. Because of these factors—especially the last—as other regions open to foreign investment, the pace of growth in the original SEZs may moderate somewhat.

Hainan Special Economic Zone

Hainan Island was one of the poorest regions of China through the mid-1980s, with a predominantly agricultural economy and inadequately developed infrastructure. It was designated a "special area open to foreign investment" in 1983, but initially it remained unable to attract foreign investment mainly because of the lack of infrastructure. However, as labor became increasingly expensive in Guangdong, Hainan became an important source of cheap labor in southern China. This development, together with its land and natural resource endowment, gave it some comparative advantage for foreign investment in labor-intensive activities.

In 1988, Hainan was designated as China's largest SEZ (it was also given the status of a province) and began to focus more on attracting foreign investment and on export production. It benefited from low land prices, cheap labor costs, and the free movement of capital and merchandise, and in some respects its preferential policies were more generous than those of the other SEZs. For instance, to develop its infrastructure (ports, airports, roads, railways, coal mining, and power plants), special income tax incentives were offered. In 1992, the State Council

---

[63]Considerable variation is found in the data derived from various sources on open economic zones. An extended time series of industrial output at constant prices is not available.

[64]A summary of incentives offered in selected countries appears in Table 11.

approved measures to develop Yangpu port in Hainan to attract foreign investment into the development of land in the area.[65]

Hainan was also one of the regions in which experiments with a decentralized and market-oriented approach to economic management—now spreading across China—were carried out, and its need to develop an adequate infrastructure influenced the nature of the measures that it introduced. Its authorities were empowered to approve projects that meet specified conditions and whose total investment is less than $30 million, and it can issue bonds with the approval of the State Council. It was one of the few areas where foreign exchange earnings could be retained in cash regardless of ownership,[66] and where foreigners could purchase stocks and bonds before this operation was allowed in other parts of China. Trading in land use rights (for leases of up to 70 years) was also first permitted there. Domestic and foreign investors were allowed to set up companies to develop large tracts of land.

During 1988–91, Hainan's economic development accelerated and its per capita income caught up with the rest of China. By the end of 1991, it had approved the establishment of more than 2,000 FFEs with investment contracts amounting to $394 million and actual investment of $176 million. Financial resources from other provinces amounted to Y 4.2 billion. Although its trade performance was strong during this period—exports increased from $281 million to $670 million—they remained a relatively small proportion of GDP (less than the national average) and were concentrated in primary products. Although another large increase appears to have occurred in 1992, Hainan has not yet reached the "take-off" point long since achieved by the other SEZs.

Open Coastal Cities

The success of the original four SEZs led to the authorities' decision in April 1984 to open 14 coastal cities[67] to foreign trade and investment. At the time of their selection, the 14 coastal cities had already developed significant industrial bases and adequate infrastructure and possessed technical and managerial expertise. The authorities of the cities were given the power to approve construction and industrial projects involving foreign investment not exceeding $5 million.[68] Nonmanufacturing projects involving foreign investment are not subject to upper limits but must be mainly financed by foreign resources.

The open coastal cities are classified into two parts for the purposes of incentives: the economic and technical development zones (ETDZs) and the rest of the cities. The ETDZs are often located near the harbor and are designed to provide the basic infrastructure for the establishment of new enterprises. They enjoy the same tax concessions as those offered in SEZs (for example, a 15 percent income tax rate and tax holidays), although exemptions from import duties apply only to capital equipment and intermediate goods and not to consumer goods. In the other parts of the cities, the corporate income tax is set at an intermediate rate of 24 percent except for high-technology projects and investment projects exceeding $30 million, or projects in the energy, transportation, and port construction sectors, which are eligible for rates as low as 15 percent.

The economic performance of the 14 coastal cities has varied. Although 8 recorded growth rates of industrial output higher than the national average, the average growth rate of the 14 cities taken as a group is estimated to have been well below the national average in 1984–91. This is largely because Shanghai and Tianjin, the two largest industrial cities, grew at relatively low rates—6.7 and 8.5 percent, respectively—compared with the national average of 12.1 percent (Table 8). In these cities preferential policies would have had a more limited impact because the ETDZs were small relative to the overall size of the cities.

Measured by external aggregates, the open coastal cities performed well; for instance, the value of foreign direct investment grew by nearly 35 percent in 1991 and increased threefold in 1992. By the early 1990s, they were absorbing about one-fourth of China's foreign direct investment, and their export/GDP ratios averaged over 100 percent; although these statistics include trade originating in other provinces, they indicate the importance of the cities in the overall process of opening.[69]

At first glance, there is a contradiction between the rapid growth of exports and the slow development of industrial production in the 14 open coastal cities. This difference in relative performance re-

---

[65]The maximum area of land to be leased for development is 30 square kilometers at a time. The land use rights can be leased out, mortgaged, or used as equity contribution in setting up a joint venture.

[66]See SRI International Associates Program, *China's Regions Emerge* (Beijing, September 1992), p. 13.

[67]From north to south, Dalian, Qinhuangdao, Tianjin, Yantai, Qingdao, Lianyungang, Nantong, Shanghai, Ningbo, Wenzhou, Fuzhou, Guangzhou, Zhanjian, and Beihai.

[68]In 1984, this limit was set at $10 million for Dalian and $30 million for Tianjin and Shanghai.

[69]The statistics also refer to the total exports of each open coastal city, and not to that of the ETDZ, which could have witnessed a considerably higher growth rate.

flects the concentration of new activity in export-oriented production, the relatively low base of exports, and the large existing industrial base. It also indicates that the principal objective of the preferential terms offered in the ETDZs has been to increase exports. Finally, the expansion of industrial production in older cities such as Shanghai and Tianjin requires overhauling large and inefficient state-owned enterprises and undertaking extensive renovation of infrastructure. Neither of these could be fully addressed by inflows of foreign direct investment, in part reflecting the ambivalence of the authorities on the extent of foreign involvement in the restructuring of SOEs.

Pudong New Area

A further step in the policy of opening up—the most ambitious single undertaking by far—came in April 1990 with the establishment of the Pudong New Area of Shanghai. It was designated an open economic zone that would enjoy a policy status more flexible than those already applied in the original SEZs and that would from the outset be much more integrated with the surrounding region. Pudong was expected to take the lead in the development and opening of the Yangtze River valley and to be the focal point in China's development during the 1990s. The authorities envisaged that, by this means, Shanghai would become a major economic, trading, and financial center for China, and indeed for the entire Asian region.

At the time of its selection, Pudong was already different from the original four SEZs in that it was not to be developed from scratch on virgin land. Its development was to be strongly supported by Puxi, the western part of Shanghai. Pudong's development aims were to establish a finance and trade zone, an export processing zone, a free trade zone, and a high-technology park. Its preferential policies were broader in scope than those of the original SEZs, and the municipality expected strong financial support from both public and private sources in developing the infrastructure of the area.

The distinctive features of activities permitted in Pudong (many of which were subsequently extended to other OEZs) included (1) foreign business was allowed to engage in retail sales; (2) all foreign-owned enterprises could trade their foreign exchange freely; (3) foreign insurance companies could be established; (4) foreign enterprises could build and operate port facilities; (5) authorization was given to establish a free trade zone (Waigaoqiao) in which approved enterprises could engage in foreign trade freely without restriction; and (6) a securities market was opened with the approval of

the People's Bank of China.[70] In most other respects, Pudong offered incentives similar to those already available in Hainan and the original SEZs. However, unlike Hainan, where both domestic and foreign-funded enterprises enjoy preferential treatment, Pudong originally offered incentives only to the latter.[71]

Although still in its infancy, early results from Pudong were encouraging.[72] The area attracted numerous foreign and domestic investors, many of whom invested in high-technology industries rather than the more basic light industries that characterized the other open zones. From 1990 to 1992, approvals were given for 704 foreign-funded projects with a total investment of more than $3 billion; projects have included electronics, chemicals, telecommunications, precision and measuring instruments, microbiology, and automobile parts. Eleven branches of foreign banks have been established, and over 30 other banks have applied to open branches in Pudong.

Domestic investment is also on the rise. More than 1,000 enterprises had been set up by the central, provincial, and municipal governments by the end of 1992 involving a commitment of investment of Y 8.5 billion. In 1991, Pudong made its first six land deals, covering an area of 964 hectares.[73] Business in other areas also developed quickly in 1990–92. For example, the value of securities transacted on the Shanghai stock exchange was Y 2.4 billion in 1990; it increased to Y 12.6 billion in 1991 and to Y 68 billion in 1992.

Inland Provinces

Foreign investment in inland provinces[74] was relatively low from 1978 through 1991. Foreign direct investment projects, which were predominantly resource-based ventures, were concentrated in a few areas including Beijing and a number of cities in Shaanxi and Sichuan.

---

[70]Currently the market is physically in the older western part of Shanghai, but the intention is to move it to Pudong.

[71]Enterprises in Hainan do not have to apply for tax exemptions once their projects have been approved, whereas in Pudong they must apply separately for tax-exempt status.

[72]Official estimates of GNP point to growth of about 14 percent in 1991 compared with 7.7 percent for China as a whole.

[73]Prices for land use rights were fixed by the Shanghai government: $900 a square meter for the first tract of land for nonindustrial use, but the price for industrial development was held to $100 a square meter. In both cases the term was for 50 years.

[74]Inland provinces are all provinces not considered coastal provinces. The coastal provinces are Liaoning, Tianjin, Hebei, Shandong, Jiangsu, Shanghai, Zhejiang, Fujian, Guangdong, Guangxi, and Hainan.

Although foreign trade from inland provinces developed faster than foreign direct investment, it still lagged far behind that of the coastal provinces, particularly the open coastal cities. In 1990, exports and imports from the inland provinces accounted for about 28 and 10 percent of the national total, respectively. The trade/GNP ratio of the inland provinces was 12.3 percent in 1990, while that of the coastal provinces was close to 40 percent.[75]

One important factor in keeping foreign direct investment low in inland provinces is that they were at a disadvantage in terms of tax policy. Income tax on net profits of foreign-funded enterprises was unified in 1991 at 30 percent plus a 3 percent local surtax.[76] Until that time tax rates for joint ventures had differed from those for wholly foreign-owned enterprises. Other factors that had discouraged foreign investment in inland provinces included local governments' limited power to approve investment projects;[77] poor infrastructure (particularly transportation and communications); and lack of managerial expertise and skilled labor and inadequate research and development.

Despite their dependence on domestic demand, the average annual economic growth in the inland provinces was very close to that of the open coastal areas during 1984–90. Among the many factors that may have contributed was the improvement in the terms of trade of the inland provinces relative to the coastal areas. The domestic prices of energy and raw materials have continued to rise in recent years, exceeding the price increases in manufactured goods. This is to the advantage of the inland provinces, which supply primary products to coastal areas.

In 1992, the authorities embarked on a new phase of the process of opening up. The central government decided to apply preferential policies to ten major cities and to establish six development zones along the Yangtze River valley.[78] The Government also gave permission to all provincial capitals and to 13 border cities to adopt similar policies of opening up.[79] In the cities along the Yangtze River, the strategy is to integrate their development with that of the Pudong region in Shanghai. Most of the incentives offered in the original SEZs, Hainan, and Pudong are to be applied in the newly opened cities of inland provinces.

In addition to those inland and border areas officially sanctioned by the central authorities, many localities have announced plans to set up development zones without awaiting approval from the central authorities. As well as the existing packages of incentives offered by the central government, provinces have further devolved their powers to local authorities under their jurisdiction to approve foreign investment projects in their respective areas. Some of the areas have adopted more generous policies than those applied in SEZs and Pudong without approval from the central government. Such terms include a five-year tax exemption and a 50 percent reduction of corporate income tax over the next five years and exemption from the energy transportation tax to foreign-funded enterprises.

Review of Progress

There have been two broad strata of policies—at the national level and at the regional level—through which China has gradually opened its economy to the rest of the world. Each contains transitional elements that indicate that lasting reform will require further substantial changes in policy orientation.

At the national level, there has clearly been substantial progress in liberalizing the trade and exchange regimes, but they remain distorted and lacking in transparency. The swap market has provided a market-oriented mechanism of allocating foreign exchange for imports that are outside the foreign exchange plan. It has also relaxed the foreign exchange constraint for foreign investors wishing to invest in China because they can now satisfy their foreign exchange requirements through the swap market. This has facilitated the large inflows of foreign capital into the service sector during the past year.

However, exchange rate developments in 1993 underscore the need to extend market-based mechanisms for determining the exchange rate to all transactions. The authorities have announced their intention to reform the foreign exchange system to

---

[75]The external trade of the inland provinces may be underestimated by the statistics, which tend to report transactions according to the location of foreign trading corporations that handle the trade rather than the producing enterprises that are often located in inland provinces.

[76]This rate is double that applied in SEZs and ETDZs, as well as on targeted projects in other parts of the 14 open coastal cities.

[77]Unlike the OEZs where the project approval limit was $30 million, the inland provincial authorities could approve projects only up to $5 million.

[78]The ten cities are Nanjing and Zhejian (Jiangsu province); Wuhu, Tanglin, Angin, and Maanshang (Anhui province); Jiujiang (Jiangxi province); Yueyan (Hunan province); Wuhan (Hubei province); and Chongqing (Sichuan province). The six zones are Shanghai-Nanjing zone, the Wuhan development zone, the Hunan-Hubei-Jiangxi zone, the Chongqing-Yichang zone, the Wujiang hydropower and mineral resource development zone, and the Panxi-Luipanshui comprehensive resource development zone.

[79]In addition, trade and other economic cooperation between China's border provinces and Russia, Mongolia, Myanmar, India, and Viet Nam are being encouraged, and many administrative restrictions are being eliminated. Many provinces also announced their own plans to open more border cities.

Box 6. The Impact on the Economy of Opening Up: Selected Features

This box reviews selected facets of developments in the Chinese economy resulting from the policy of opening up: from an overall perspective, from the perspective of the province most affected (Guangdong), and from the perspective of the most dynamic sector of the economy.

National

The impact of the more rapid opening up in 1992 had a tangible effect on a number of key statistics for China as a whole. The value of exports in 1992 increased by over 18 percent to $85 billion, with the proportion of manufactured goods rising to 80 percent of total exports. Of this total, the exports by FFEs rose from 17 percent in 1991 to about 20 percent in 1992. Contracted foreign direct investment actually used was $11.2 billion, an increase of 150 percent over 1991. At the same time, the number of FFEs rose from 37,000 at the end of 1991 to 84,000 a year later.

Guangdong

The impact of the policy on open economic zones is clearly illustrated by developments in Guangdong province, where the first three SEZs were established. Apart from these SEZs, Guangdong has 2 of the 14 open coastal cities and the Pearl River Delta Zone of Economic Development, which includes 10 cities and 29 counties. Guangdong's export volume increased by over 19 percent annually during 1979–91, and the province as a whole utilized $15 billion of foreign capital and imported sizable amounts of advanced technology. By the end of 1992, there were 16,000 foreign-funded enterprises—including joint ventures—operating in Guangdong. Although Guangdong is the province that has the largest concentration of foreign investment, similar developments have been recorded in most other open zones—an indication of the extent to which the policy of opening to the rest of the world has contributed to the rapid development of China's economy.

Nonstate Industries

The share of town and village enterprises in total exports reportedly increased fivefold between 1985 and 1990 and is estimated to be in excess of 25 percent in 1992. About 90 percent of TVE exports are estimated to be manufactures, of which almost half are spread evenly among textiles, clothing, and arts and crafts. The bulk of all TVE export earnings are generated in the eastern coastal provinces/municipalities. Available data for foreign-funded enterprises (including joint ventures) indicate that their contribution to exports rose from 1 percent in 1984 to 5 percent in 1988 and to 10 percent in 1990. All their exports are of manufactured goods, and 94 percent are generated in the coastal provinces.

achieve eventual convertibility of the currency. Their plans include establishing an integrated national swap market; replacing retention in quotas with cash retention; and unifying the official and swap rates.

At the regional level, despite the increasing number and macroeconomic significance of the open zones, two questions on their future may be highlighted. Present domestic policies have created competition among the various provinces to offer the most generous incentives to investors without due regard to the possible adverse impact on government revenue. In addition, concerns have arisen that the proliferation of development zones could divert land from agricultural use, a critical issue given the relative scarcity of arable land. Partly because of these concerns, the Government has slowed the opening of development zones.[80] In the longer term, it may become necessary for the authorities to review the policy of offering preferential terms to new investors in these zones.

Whatever the future of China's open economic zones, there can be little doubt that they have played an important role in transforming China into a market economy (Box 6). They have gone far beyond their initial goals of attracting foreign investment and technology and of earning foreign exchange to procure imports to modernize the economy. Their use as laboratories for experimenting with market-oriented policies and the gradual spread of the various forms of zones have established them as nodes of development that are influencing changes in other parts of the country.

As the Chinese economy becomes more market oriented and open, the time will come for a careful review of the role of such zones. A key question in that context would be whether China's long-term development is best served by phasing out those special arrangements that should be regarded as transitional (such as certain tax concessions) while extending others to all parts of the country.

---

[80]Estimates of newly opened development zones since the beginning of 1992 at and above county level reached 1,800, and the number of zones at all levels (including township and village) was as high as 9,000.

V Decentralization and Regional Development

China's regional policy has been crucial in stimulating reform and, by the same token, high regional growth rates have contributed to the macroeconomic imbalances that have periodically developed. Analysis of the role of the central policies toward certain regions and of the policies pursued by regional governments is complicated not only because of the size and complexity of the economy but also because of the speed with which policy changes have occurred, particularly in 1992 and 1993.

Although there were several phases of decentralization and recentralization in the period before 1979, the regional pattern of development and hence the growth performance of the regions were largely determined by central direction and were subject to nationwide priorities. Since the late 1970s, decentralization—under which local authorities and enterprises acquired increasingly greater autonomy in fiscal resource allocation, investment, production, and trade—has linked each province's development more directly with its own resource endowment and priorities.

This section examines the major factors that influenced the performance of the provinces as decentralization proceeded in the context of the reforms since 1978. These include changes in the orientation of central government policy, ownership structure, and financial relations between the center and the provinces. Appendix II contains some empirical analysis of the major determinants of provincial and regional differences in growth. Considerable attention is paid to financial relations—which include fiscal and credit policies as well as issues of foreign trade and investment—because of their importance for the conduct of macroeconomic policy. China's progress toward a more market-oriented economy has heightened the need to rely on indirect methods of macroeconomic management. At the same time, decentralization has involved institutional changes that have impaired the capacity of the Government to implement these methods.

Policy Orientation: Industrial or Regional?

Considerable debate has taken place over the orientation of policy in the period since 1978. A certain ambivalence by the authorities arose from their conflicting goals of opening the economy while attempting to ensure an equitable distribution of the benefits of economic growth, and of developing an "appropriate" industrial structure. Prior to the late 1980s, the focus on export-led growth in specific localities gave rise to strong cross-regional policy differentials, widely referred to as the "regional tilt" policy. However, policy during this period was not completely free of an "industrial tilt," although the term "industrial policy" was not officially used until 1989.

In the late 1970s, two strands of central government policy combined to create conditions that were favorable for the development of new industries in certain coastal provinces, thereby setting a pattern of development that would help these provinces. First, priority was accorded to light industry and agriculture to redress the previous imbalance toward heavy industry. Second, as the open-door policy was initiated, the export-oriented and technologically advanced industries were given precedence in various regulations, notably those issued in October 1986 by the State Council, designed to provide additional incentives to foreign investors.

Debate over the orientation of policy intensified during 1988–90 as the perception grew that cross-regional differences in absolute income and growth rates were widening. Moreover, increasing interregional trade barriers and other monopolistic practices also increased concerns about the distorting effects of regional policy.

Against this background, an industrial policy containing a detailed list of favored and restricted sectors was for the first time formally promulgated by the State Council in 1989. Initially, the most frequently used measures to implement industrial policy were administrative restrictions through investment approval procedures and the credit plan, although there was some indirect use of the market mechanism, through interest and tax rate differentials. In 1991, the State Council converted the construction tax into an investment direction adjustment tax. Previously, investments in basic construction were subject to a unified construction tax rate, whereas after the revision differential rates were applied to projects with different ranks of priority. Although most of these policies differentiated among industries, in at least one important respect the move away from a regional tilt resulted in a more level "playing field": the considerable simplification that took place in the foreign exchange retention scheme (see Section IV), which largely eliminated any regional or industrial bias in the retention of export earnings. The opening of inland provinces since early 1992 has represented a further move away from the regional tilt policy.

Despite the shift toward an industrial policy, there has been little impact on industrial structure and regional resource allocation. The central government has not only shifted its priorities—toward infrastructure rather than heavy industry—but has fundamentally altered its role in resource allocation; in particular, mandatory planning is being rapidly phased out in favor of more indirect methods. As a result, central government priorities have been overridden by those of the provincial authorities—especially in the coastal regions—as they have progressively acquired more autonomy. Moreover, there have been a number of new regionally oriented policy initiatives since 1988, including those in Hainan, Pudong, and the opening of the inland and border areas.

Evolution of Ownership Structure

Since decentralization has proceeded along with the change in ownership structure, the latter is a significant indicator of a region's progress toward reform. During the early years of decentralization, many centrally owned SOEs—and more importantly areas of economic activity—were transferred to the jurisdiction of the provinces.[81] Given this more decentralized system, each province acquired greater potential to determine its own priorities and policies and thereby to influence its own performance, including the extent to which it promoted collectives (especially the dynamic TVEs) and private enterprises.

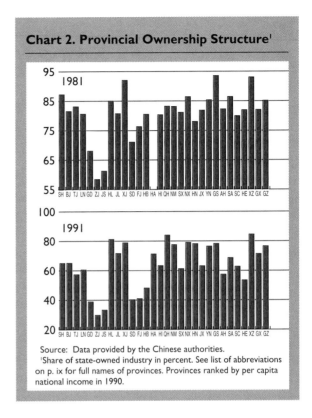

Chart 2. Provincial Ownership Structure[1]

Source: Data provided by the Chinese authorities.
[1]Share of state-owned industry in percent. See list of abbreviations on p. ix for full names of provinces. Provinces ranked by per capita national income in 1990.

Nevertheless, the central government still influences ownership structure in the provinces in at least two ways. First, many SOEs are still directly under central control, and thus reform can proceed only at the pace permitted by the center. Second, some provinces continue to have a high concentration of SOEs either because of their endowments of raw materials or because they have traditionally been centers of heavy industry.

Although there has clearly been a reduction in state ownership during the reform era, the pace at which the ownership structure has changed has differed across provinces (Chart 2). For instance, between 1981 and 1991, the share of state-owned industry in total industrial output fell in the coastal province of Zhejiang from 58 percent to 29 percent, while in the interior province of Qinghai, it had stayed virtually unchanged at 83 percent. This growing diversity is reflected in a statistical measure of the share of SOEs in total industrial output: the coefficient of variation[82] rose from only 0.097—reflecting a highly uniform ownership structure—to 0.24 in 1991.

The fastest growing provinces—including Zhe-

---

[81]As explained in Section II, the state sector consists of SOEs owned by the central and provincial authorities, whereas the nonstate sector comprises collectives, private enterprises, and foreign-funded enterprises.

[82]Defined as standard deviation/mean and designed to measure the extent of dispersion among observations in two or more series with different means. Low values reflect a less diverse or more homogeneous set of observations.

jiang, Jiangsu, Guangdong, Fujian, and Shandong—are those in which the share of state-owned industry has fallen most sharply. By 1991, the share of the SOEs in each of these five provinces had fallen by almost half, to about 30–40 percent, creating a structure dominated by the nonstate sector. By contrast, the remote (mainly western) provinces experienced a much lower pace of change. For instance, Qinghai, Guizhou, Ningxia, Inner Mongolia, and Heilongjiang all saw a decline of less than 10 percentage points, with the share of SOEs in industrial output staying at over 75 percent.

The growth of the nonstate sector took on slightly different forms in various provinces: TVEs (Jiangsu and Zhejiang), foreign-funded enterprises (Guangdong), and private enterprises (Zhejiang). Among these, the most significant development was the growth of the TVEs mainly in the coastal provinces. From 1978 to 1991, the nationwide output by TVEs grew at an annual average rate of 22 percent, 14 percentage points higher than that of the state-owned industrial enterprises.[83] In 1991, 70 percent of the total sales revenue of TVEs came from the 12 coastal provinces and municipalities, with only 8 percent from the 9 western provinces and autonomous regions. Not only did the output growth of the TVEs exceed that of the SOEs, but their higher rate of productivity growth shows the stronger potential for growth of the TVEs.[84]

Center-Local Financial Relations[85]

Fiscal Relations

The fiscal relationship between the central and local governments has been a major source of tension as decentralization has proceeded. Before 1980, all revenues were remitted to the central government and then transferred back to the provinces according to expenditure needs approved by the center. Since the early 1980s, this relationship has gone through three major changes.[86]

In 1980, a revenue-sharing arrangement was established under which there were three basic types of taxes: those accruing to the center, those accruing to the localities, and revenue that was shared between the center and localities according to agreed formulas. During 1980–84, about 80 percent of the shared revenue was remitted to the central government and 20 percent remained with the local governments. This arrangement resulted in surpluses in wealthy provinces and deficits in poor provinces.

In 1985, a new arrangement—intended to create incentives for revenue collection by each province—set varying schedules based on each locality's budget balance in the previous year. However, the central government continued to maintain a tight grip over the highest revenue-yielding regions, including Shanghai, Beijing, Tianjin, Liaoning, Jiangsu, and Zhejiang.

In 1988, a fiscal contract system was adopted, in which six types of revenue sharing were introduced (Table 12).[87] This system further increased the revenue share retained by the localities, particularly the major contributors to the central government's revenue. When the initial three-year contracts expired in 1990, it proved impossible to negotiate satisfactory replacements; as a result the first generation of contracts has been repeatedly extended pending the negotiation of alternative arrangements. In 1992, experiments with a system of separate taxation were begun in nine provinces/municipalities.

In practice, the fiscal contracts were subject to continuing renegotiation usually to the disadvantage of the central government. For instance, in 1990 only 6 provinces recorded a surplus (Chart 3), even though 16 were contractually obliged to do so.[88] Thus, the central authorities have frequently expressed concerns as to the distribution or assignment of resources between the center and localities and the difficulty of maintaining sufficient control over total fiscal expenditure.

---

[83]A similar phenomenon can be observed in other nonstate industry. In 1991, the 12 coastal provinces and municipalities accounted for over 70 percent of total industrial output by domestic private enterprises and "other" (mainly foreign-funded) enterprises, while the 9 western provinces and autonomous regions accounted for only 8 percent.

[84]Ma and Kim (1992) compare the performance of the SOEs and TVEs using a Tornqvist-Theil TFP index (in which input shares are averaged by data at the beginning and end periods). Between 1978 and 1990, the TFP average annual growth rate of the TVEs was 9.1 percent, compared with 1.0 percent for the SOEs.

[85]The statistical analysis in this section is based largely on data for 1990, the most recent year for which comparable cross-province data are available. Subsequent developments and policy shifts are likely to have caused some, possibly major, changes in certain variables discussed here.

---

[86]Li, Li, and Ma (1989), Oksenberg and Tong (1991), and World Bank (1993b) have described in detail the evolution of China's center-local fiscal relations since 1980.

[87]These contracts apply only to that part of revenue shared between the center and local governments. Three provinces (Shanghai, Heilongjiang, and Jiangsu) still provide the lion's share of the budgetary surpluses. Guangdong is notable among the higher-income provinces in running a deficit.

[88]An example of this is provided by Henan province, which in 1990 was contracted to transfer Y 1.4 billion to the center out of total collections of Y 8.4 billion. However, this amount was reduced by additional subsidies for enterprise losses (including foreign trading corporations) and grain, disaster relief, and additional capital construction. In the end, the central government transferred Y 0.4 billion to Henan (see World Bank, 1993a).

Table 12. Central-Local Resource-Sharing Contracts, 1988–92[1]

| | Type A[2] Variable Retention by Formula | | Type B | Type C Variable Remittance by Formula | | Type D Semi-Fixed Amounts to State | | Type E | |
	Contracted rate of increase (In percent)	Local retention rate (In percent)	Fixed Rate of Retention (In percent)	Basic remittance to center (In percent)	Marginal remittance (In percent)	Initial amount to state (Y 100 million)	Contracted annual rate of increase (In percent)	Fixed Amount to State (Y 100 million)	Contracted Transfers to Provinces (Y 10 million)
Beijing	4.0	50.0	…	…	…	…	…	…	…
Hebei	4.5	70.0	…	…	…	…	…	…	…
Liaoning	3.5	58.3	…	…	…	…	…	…	…
Shenyang	4.0	30.3	…	…	…	…	…	…	…
Harbin	5.0	45.0	…	…	…	…	…	…	…
Jiangsu	5.0	41.0	…	…	…	…	…	…	…
Zhejiang	6.5	61.5	…	…	…	…	…	…	…
Ningbo	5.3	27.9	…	…	…	…	…	…	…
Henan	5.0	80.0	…	…	…	…	…	…	…
Chongqing[3]	4.0	33.5	…	…	…	…	…	…	…
Tianjin	…	…	46.5	…	…	…	…	…	…
Shanxi	…	…	87.6	…	…	…	…	…	…
Anhui	…	…	77.5	…	…	…	…	…	…
Dalian	…	…	…	27.7	27.3	…	…	…	…
Qingdao	…	…	…	16.0	34.0	…	…	…	…
Wuhan[3]	…	…	…	17.0	25.0	…	…	…	…
Guangdong (including Guangzhou)	…	…	…	…	…	14.1	9.0	…	…
Hunan	…	…	…	…	…	8.0	7.0	…	…
Shanghai	…	…	…	…	…	…	…	105.0	…
Shandong	…	…	…	…	…	…	…	2.9	…
Heilongjiang	…	…	…	…	…	…	…	3.0	…
Jilin	…	…	…	…	…	…	…	…	1.1
Jiangxi	…	…	…	…	…	…	…	…	0.5
Shaanxi (including Xian)	…	…	…	…	…	…	…	…	1.2
Gansu	…	…	…	…	…	…	…	…	1.3
Fujian (beginning 1989)	…	…	…	…	…	…	…	…	0.5
Inner Mongolia	…	…	…	…	…	…	…	…	18.4
Guangxi-Zhuang	…	…	…	…	…	…	…	…	6.1
Tibet Autonomous Region of China	…	…	…	…	…	…	…	…	9.0
Ningxia-hui	…	…	…	…	…	…	…	…	5.3
Xinjiang-uygur	…	…	…	…	…	…	…	…	15.3
Guizhou	…	…	…	…	…	…	…	…	7.4
Yunnan	…	…	…	…	…	…	…	…	6.7
Qinghai	…	…	…	…	…	…	…	…	6.6
Hainan	…	…	…	…	…	…	…	…	1.4

Source: Ministry of Finance.

[1] These contracts were intended to cover three years but have been extended annually in subsequent years.

[2] The locality retained a specified proportion (local retention rate) of any revenue that was less than or equal to the contracted rate of increase. Any revenue above this amount was retained locally.

[3] After the cities of Wuhan and Chongqing were separated from Hubei and Sichuan provinces, the provinces changed from net providers to the state to net recipients of subsidies from the state. The difference between their expenditures and their income, which was made up from income that Wuhan and Chongqing sent to the provinces, served as central government subsidies to the local governments. The percentage that Wuhan and Chongqing gave to the provinces was 4.8 percent and 10.7 percent, respectively.

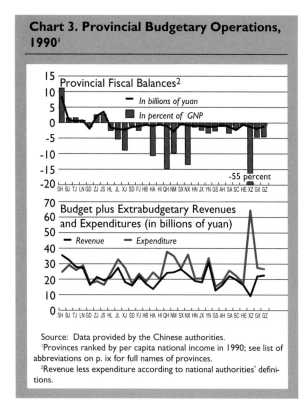

Chart 3. Provincial Budgetary Operations, 1990[1]

Source: Data provided by the Chinese authorities.
[1]Provinces ranked by per capita national income in 1990; see list of abbreviations on p. ix for full names of provinces.
[2]Revenue less expenditure according to national authorities' definitions.

Although most fiscal revenue is collected by local agencies, it is—at least in principle—designated as central, local, or shared. Through much of the reform era, this distribution of revenue has derived from the ownership of the enterprises that generate the revenue. As Wong (1991) points out, through the 1980s the central government actually increased the proportion of its claims on total resources by various means including the appropriation of some of the most profitable enterprises (in industries such as automobiles, tobacco, petrochemicals, and shipping); the introduction of taxes on extrabudgetary funds of enterprises; and the recentralization in 1985 of four key sectors—coal, nonferrous metals, petroleum, and power. However, this development has been offset by another effect of decentralization: the localities now "own" many of the more recently established enterprises and derive substantial income directly from this source.

In summary, these developments have been reflected in the various trends illustrated in Table 13, which include (1) a gradual decline in the total revenue/GNP ratio that reflected a parallel fall in the central revenue/GDP ratio; (2) an increase in the local revenue/GNP ratio through the mid-1980s and a decline thereafter; and (3) a marked decline in the share of revenue collected through local taxes (before tax-sharing), accompanied by an increase in the share retained by the localities. It is this last charac-

teristic, which has led to a sharp reduction in the relative size of transfers from the localities to the center, that is at the heart of the central government's concerns.

Although the resources available to the localities have indeed grown, the demands for expenditure placed upon them have also increased, arguably disproportionately—leading to attempts by localities to mobilize other sources of revenue to meet all their obligations. The proportion of total expenditure financed by the center declined through much of the 1980s as the provinces were expected to assume greater responsibility for social, health, and education expenditures and for the financing of some elements of subsidies. The center no longer explicitly stipulates the specific expenditures, but the policies of the central government determine the nature of the expenditure commitments of the local authorities.

Credit Policy

In the first phase of financial reform through the mid-1980s, the People's Bank of China—until then a monobank—was broken into a number of specialized banks, with the People's Bank retaining the function of the central bank.[89] Each major bank, including the People's Bank, shares an organizational structure that parallels the Government's administrative structure, with the national headquarters at the top, provincial and municipal branches in the middle, and the city/county branches at the bottom.

At present, the influence of the People's Bank is circumscribed by a system of "dual leadership."[90] At the national level, its power is limited, since it is answerable to the State Council in a capacity similar to other line ministries. At the provincial level, its branches are administratively linked to local governments; the authority of the center was strengthened in 1988 through a decision to allow the headquarters of the People's Bank to appoint provincial bank presidents.

There is a close relationship between People's Bank lending to specialized banks and the allocation of credit among provinces, reflecting national priorities for the regional distribution of resources. Indeed, the demarcation between the credit and fiscal policies is often blurred by decisions—proposed

---

[89]In addition, there are two comprehensive banks, an ever-increasing number of nonbank financial institutions, and a large network of rural credit cooperatives (whose supervision is delegated to the Agricultural Bank of China) and urban credit cooperatives.

[90]See World Bank (1990b) for a more complete description of the institutional characteristics of the Chinese banking system.

Table 13. Central and Local Revenues[1]

	1979	1980	1981	1982	1983	1984	1985	1986	1987	1988	1989	1990	1991
							(In percent of GNP)						
Revenue before tax sharing	26.7	23.3	21.3	20.0	20.1	20.6	20.7	21.9	19.5	16.8	16.7	16.6	15.8
Central	3.1	2.9	3.2	3.4	5.0	6.5	7.2	8.0	6.5	5.5	5.2	5.6	4.6
Local	23.6	20.4	18.1	16.7	15.1	14.1	13.5	13.9	12.9	11.3	11.6	11.0	11.1
Revenue after tax sharing	26.7	23.3	21.3	20.0	20.1	20.6	20.7	21.9	19.5	16.8	16.7	16.6	15.8
Central	...	...	12.5	10.3	10.1	10.9	10.2	10.4	9.4	7.4	7.1	7.5	...
Local	...	...	8.8	9.7	10.0	9.7	10.5	11.5	10.1	9.4	9.7	9.1	...
Net payment shared from local to central level	...	...	9.3	6.3	5.1	3.2	3.0	3.5	3.6	1.9	1.9	1.9	...
							(In percent of total revenue)						
Revenue before tax sharing	100.0	100.0	100.0	100.0	100.0	100.0	100.0	100.0	100.0	100.0	100.0	100.0	100.0
Central	11.4	12.6	15.0	16.8	25.0	31.4	34.8	36.7	33.5	32.9	30.9	33.8	29.3
Local	88.6	87.5	85.0	83.2	75.0	68.6	65.2	63.3	66.5	67.1	69.1	66.2	70.7
Revenue after tax sharing	100.0	100.0	100.0	100.0	100.0	100.0	100.0	100.0	100.0	100.0	100.0	100.0	100.0
Central	...	...	58.6	51.4	50.2	52.9	49.2	47.5	48.3	44.3	42.3	45.1	...
Local	...	...	41.5	48.7	49.7	47.1	50.7	52.5	51.7	55.7	57.7	54.9	...
Memorandum items:							*(In percent of GNP)*						
Total extra budgetary receipts	11.3	12.5	12.6	15.5	16.7	17.2	17.9	17.9	18.0	16.8	16.7	15.3	...
Central	...	...	...	5.2	6.2	6.8	7.4	7.4	7.3	6.5	6.7	6.1	...
Local	...	...	...	10.2	10.5	10.4	10.4	10.5	10.6	10.4	10.0	9.2	...
Budgetary plus extra budgetary[2]	38.0	35.8	33.9	35.5	36.8	37.8	38.6	39.8	37.5	33.6	33.4	31.9	...
Central	...	...	...	15.5	16.3	17.7	18.6	17.8	16.7	13.9	13.8	13.6	...
Local	...	...	...	19.9	20.5	20.1	20.9	22.0	20.7	19.8	19.7	18.3	...

Source: World Bank (1993a).
[1] Excluding the proceeds of debt issue.
[2] After revenue sharing.

largely by the State Planning Commission—as to the proportions of investment that should be financed by the budget and the credit plan. Chart 4 illustrates that through the allocation of credit, the authorities had sought to secure sizable resource transfers from a relatively few surplus provinces (predominantly higher-income provinces) to the larger number of provinces in which growth of deposits was insufficient to finance the expansion of credit.[91] By this means a relatively even distribution of credit growth could be achieved, at least during periods such as 1990 when domestic demand was restrained.

Credit policy in a province may offset the stance of the fiscal contract. For instance, in 1991 Shanghai, which makes large fiscal transfers to the center, was allowed to expand credit by more than the increase in its deposits (Chart 4). In contrast, much tighter credit policy was imposed on Guangdong—which faces a relatively light fiscal obligation to the center—despite the strong demand for credit from this dynamic economy. Thus, even though investment in Guangdong was 80 percent higher than that in Shanghai, credit expansion was only 26 percent higher. This is striking, given that investment is clearly an important component of credit expansion.

External Policies

Of the three broad macroeconomic sectors, regional disparities are the most pronounced in the external sector. Analysis of the external financial position of the provinces is complicated by the nature of data available; a substantial proportion of external trade (particularly imports) is not recorded against the province of final use. Nevertheless,

___

[91] The financial balance in Chart 4 is the difference between the absolute increase in deposits and credit expansion during the year. The exceptionally large surplus in Beijing indicates that many enterprises maintain funds in their headquarters.

Chart 4. Provincial Monetary and Credit Operations, 1990[1]

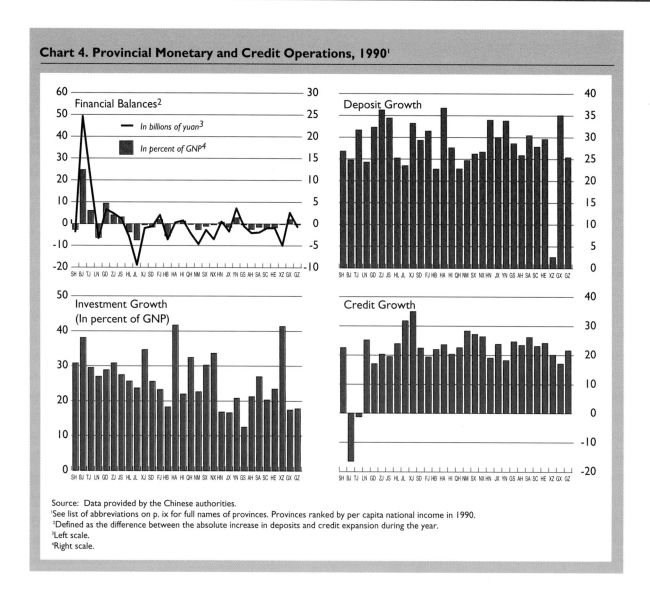

Source: Data provided by the Chinese authorities.
[1]See list of abbreviations on p. ix for full names of provinces. Provinces ranked by per capita national income in 1990.
[2]Defined as the difference between the absolute increase in deposits and credit expansion during the year.
[3]Left scale.
[4]Right scale.

available data (Chart 5) reveal that the resources generated by external trade are concentrated in a handful of coastal provinces: the highest export/GNP ratios are recorded in Shanghai, Tianjin, Liaoning, Guangdong, Jiangsu, and Shandong. However, imports in the first two provinces are substantial and leave the balance of resources created by external trade concentrated in the other four provinces. The inflow of foreign direct investment is even more heavily concentrated in one province, Guangdong, which in 1990 accounted for one-third of foreign investment inflows. By comparison, exports from Guangdong accounted for one-fifth of total exports. The large volume of external resources available to Guangdong may be one reason why the central authorities have imposed a relatively tight domestic credit policy on it, to secure the transfer of resources to other provinces.

As with other aspects of economic policies there is a hierarchical structure to the institutions involved in implementing China's external policies, all of which have undergone substantial decentralization during the reform era.[92] First, the responsibility for formulating trade policy and plans falls to the Ministry of Foreign Trade and Economic Cooperation (MOFTEC) and its commissions in each of the provinces (provincial COFTECs). Second, actual trade is conducted only by the foreign trade corporations (FTCs), incorporated at both the central and local levels, and by a growing number of producing companies that are permitted to trade on their own

---

[92]A more complete description of the evolution of China's external trade system may be found in Lardy (1992) and Panagariya (1991).

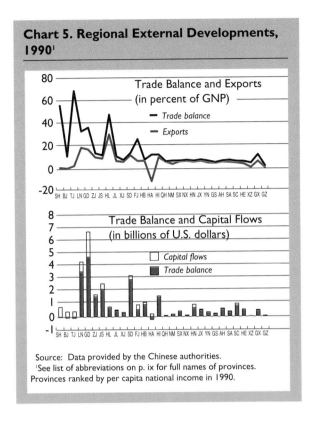

Chart 5. Regional External Developments, 1990[1]

Trade Balance and Exports (in percent of GNP)
— Trade balance
— Exports

Trade Balance and Capital Flows (in billions of U.S. dollars)
☐ Capital flows
■ Trade balance

Source: Data provided by the Chinese authorities.
[1]See list of abbreviations on p. ix for full names of provinces.
Provinces ranked by per capita national income in 1990.

account (including the foreign-funded enterprises). An indication of how extensive decentralization has been is that in 1978 foreign trade was conducted by 12 FTCs, all centrally owned; by 1991 there were some 4,000 FTCs most of which were owned at the provincial level.

Third, exchange control and external debt management are handled by the State Administration for Exchange Control (SAEC)—an agency operating under the supervision of the People's Bank of China—with branches in most localities. The SAEC controls access to the approximately 100 foreign exchange adjustment centers (or swap centers) at which the market-oriented exchange rates are set. Fourth, the bulk of foreign exchange transactions and reserve management are handled by the Bank of China (BOC) with its own extensive domestic and foreign branch network.

Until 1991, external resources were allocated between the center and localities through contractual arrangements under which remittances of foreign exchange by the latter were specified with different ratios for below- and above-plan quota amounts. Retention at the enterprise level was also differentiated according to product, and the open economic zones were permitted more favorable retention than other areas (for instance, up to 100 percent in the SEZs). The retention system was considerably sim-

plified in 1991 when a more uniform system was adopted that established formulas for the distribution of foreign exchange earnings among the center, the localities, and the enterprises.

Enterprises' retained foreign earnings can be traded in the swap centers. However, because of local protectionism, interprovincial flows of foreign exchange are restricted and the exchange rates in the swap centers tend to vary unduly. For instance, in August 1992, the premiums (the margin over the official exchange rate) in the swap centers across the country ranged from 24–36 percent. In 1992, the authorities announced their intention to establish a national exchange market and to unify the exchange rates, and they have issued regulations prohibiting local restrictions on the flow of foreign exchange. To facilitate the process, they are also planning to modernize the telecommunication facilities and payments and clearing systems.

Since direct controls have yet to be replaced by indirect instruments within an appropriate legal and regulatory framework, further risks for implementing national policies arise from growing provincial autonomy. For instance, without adequate monitoring arrangements, international trade agreements may be violated by Chinese enterprises that undertake direct negotiation with foreign counterparts. Similarly, the management of external reserves and debt is complicated by state-owned institutions under provincial authorities that undertake external borrowing or other foreign transactions (including offshore investment) without the sanction of the center while facing a soft budget constraint.

Nevertheless, the provinces remain subject to a considerable amount of central direction. First, the trade licensing and regulation system implemented by MOFTEC can be applied throughout the country on a relatively uniform basis through the network of COFTECs. Thus, in 1988/89 under the rectification program, although the number of commodities under licensing did not increase, there was an evident tightening of existing regulations in all regions, which contributed to the sharp decline in imports in 1990. Second, a much larger proportion of imports are handled by centrally owned FTCs than for exports (46 percent and 20 percent, respectively), allowing considerable scope for the implementation of import restrictions at the central level.

Third, in many cases, decentralization seems simply to have replaced direct intervention by the central government with lower levels of government—the provincial or municipal authorities. For instance, in Jiangsu province, although the center sets mandatory output targets or export quotas only for certain items, the province can set binding contracts between FTCs and the producing enterprises, which are effectively the same as mandatory targets.

The Experience of Guangdong

Guangdong covers an area of 180,000 square kilometers and has a population of 63 million (only 14 countries have a larger population). In 1978, Guangdong's per capita income was Y 313, close to the national average of Y 315, and ranked tenth among the 29 provinces, autonomous regions, and municipalities. By 1991, its per capita national income had risen to Y 2,134, ranked fifth in the country.

The Fastest Growing Region?

Guangdong is often cited as the fastest growing region in China, in Asia, and perhaps in the world. Many, including Deng Xiaoping, have sought lessons for the rest of China from Guangdong's experience. Available statistics show that while Guangdong does indeed rank consistently high in the various indices of economic growth, it is not always top, and does not outstrip other provinces by a large margin. Indeed, it has grown at a rate close to that of other coastal provinces such as Fujian, Jiangsu, Zhejiang, and Shandong in the past decade. This result arises from Guangdong's size and diversity: in addition to its well-known export-oriented light industrial base, it has an extensive agricultural sector whose performance may well have been similar to that of the rest of China.

Thus, it is not the whole province, but Southern Guangdong, or the Pearl River Delta, that has been growing strikingly fast. Unofficial estimates put average growth in many counties and cities in the Pearl River Delta at 20 percent or more in the past decade, whereas the three SEZs in the delta grew at average rates of over 30 percent. Although it would be most instructive to examine the experience of Southern Guangdong, available data restrict the analysis to the whole province.

Selected Features in Guangdong's Development

Role of Exports

Among all sectors in Guangdong, the fastest growth has come from exports. From 1978 to 1990, Guangdong's exports grew at an annual average rate of 29 percent, more than twice the province's rate of GDP growth (12.4 percent), and by 1990, total exports had reached $10.6 billion, 17 percent of the country's total. The export/GDP ratio jumped from 13 percent in 1978 to 34 percent (double the national average) in 1990. The trade surplus has consistently been about 30 percent of the value of exports or about 10 percent of GDP; even excluding consignment processing by Hong Kong companies, trade remained in surplus.

A simple decomposition of Guangdong's growth (see Appendix II) shows that during the decade through 1990, when Guangdong's average GDP growth outstripped other provinces by 3.6 percentage points, export growth contributed almost two-fifths of its growth, double the national average. As for the other sectors, their contribution to overall GDP growth was 7.7 percentage points, compared with 7.0 points for the whole of China.

Foreign Investment and Proximity to Hong Kong and Macao

Guangdong's geographic proximity and cultural and linguistic similarities have facilitated rapid economic integration with Hong Kong and Macao. Among the foreign investors in Guangdong, Hong Kong and Macao continued to be the largest source in the past decade. In most years, investment from Hong Kong and Macao has accounted for about two-thirds of the total actual foreign investment, whereas in 1991 new contracts from these territories accounted for about 90 percent of the total (Table 14). Moreover in 1991, Guangdong received 68 percent of all investment in China by Hong Kong and Macao. Guangdong is thus an extreme example of what is observed elsewhere in China—that individual provinces have concentrated on attracting investment from specific and distinct foreign countries or regions.

In addition, Hong Kong and Macao provide the primary channels that connect Guangdong's enterprises with international markets. Besides foreign direct investment, other forms of economic integration have developed, including trade, leasing, and processing and assembling. Many domestic enterprises export products through corporations in Hong Kong, and a division of labor has emerged with production shifting to the Pearl River Delta region and marketing remaining in Hong Kong. It is estimated that over 3 million people in Guangdong are now working directly or indirectly for Hong Kong-based businesses with many workers crossing the border to work in Hong Kong and vice versa.

Fiscal Relationship with the Center

Many have argued that Guangdong's rapid growth resulted from its favorable fiscal relations with the central government. Indeed, the center appears to have intentionally allowed Guangdong to remit less revenue than other provinces with comparable conditions during the past decade to give it more financial autonomy to facilitate the experiments with decentralization and reform. There was almost zero net transfer from Guangdong to the center during 1980–87, and under the 1988–91 fiscal contract Guangdong was required to submit a fixed initial

Table 14. Source of Foreign Investment in Guangdong, 1991
(In millions of U.S. dollars)

	Number of Contracted Investments	Pledged Investment	Actual Investment
Total	8,507	5,015.5	2,582.5
Hong Kong	7,623	4,229.6	1,622.8
Macao	326	248.3	102.0
Taiwan Province of China	276	263.1	115.2
Japan	49	315.1	311.8

Source: *Guangdong Statistical Yearbook*, 1992, pp. 356–58.

amount of only Y 1.4 billion with an annual growth rate of 9 percent. By contrast, Shanghai was required to submit a fixed annual amount of Y 10.5 billion. Further analysis of this question (Appendix II) suggests that the favorable fiscal relationship with the center was only a minor factor in explaining Guangdong's strong growth performance.

An Experimental Reform Zone and the Open-Door Policy

Guangdong has been used as a laboratory for various reforms and it has consistently been more aggressive in opening its economy than other provinces. Three of the four original SEZs are located in Guangdong; the Pearl River Delta Economic Development Zone was established during the mid-1980s; and eventually, in March 1988, Guangdong was designated a "comprehensive reform experiment zone" and proceeded with reforms in ten areas, including finance, fiscal matters, and trade, with the intention of further opening the region's economy. The province led the rest of China in liberalizing retail prices and removing mandatory planning.

It has also pressed the autonomy granted to the limits, seeking further concessions from the center. One striking example is that Guangdong has, with the tacit consent of the center, proceeded with investment projects that exceeded the mandate of provincial governments without central authorization. Moreover, in contrast with some other provinces, rather than centralizing authority delegated from the state in their own hands, the Guangdong authorities devolved authority further to lower levels of government (counties and cities). This devolution has enabled many productive investment projects to proceed without undue bureaucratic delays.

Can Guangdong's Experience Be Replicated?

Given that Guangdong's success has stemmed from a mixture of policies (opening the economy and reform) and geographical circumstances (especially proximity to Hong Kong and Macao), the question arises as to whether its performance can be replicated. Evidently the prospects vary according to location and natural resource endowment as well as the policy orientation of the local authorities.

Inland Provinces[93]

Many inland regions, except for some border provinces, suffer from a lack of natural trade and investment partners, poor infrastructure, inadequate managerial skill, and an inadequately trained labor force. These factors may offset any incentives that can be offered. Nonetheless, in 1992 the authorities initiated the opening of many inland areas along the Yangtze River valley, and many more localities seized the initiative to offer similar incentives without central authorization.

Priorities for these and other inland regions include drawing on the reform experience of Guangdong by allowing market forces to determine resource allocation and identify comparative advantages, encouraging nonstate enterprises, reducing government intervention, and removing interprovincial barriers to promote integration among the regions.

---

[93]There are 13 provinces that have neither a coastline nor any border with neighboring countries.

Border Provinces

China has seven provinces located along its inland borders,[94] many of which have some advantages similar to the coastal provinces in terms of international trade and economic cooperation with neighboring countries. For instance, the border prefectures and counties in Yunnan province (bordering Myanmar and Viet Nam) and whose international trade has risen sharply in recent years are reportedly among the fastest growing regions in China's border area. Northern Chinese provinces stand to benefit from trade with the former Soviet Union with its severe shortage of consumer goods. Although China's border provinces exhibit significant comparative advantages in technology and productivity relative to the inland provinces, other external factors are likely to be less favorable than in Guangdong: the neighboring countries are less developed and have smaller markets than the economies of east and southeast Asia that are providing both trade outlets and sources of capital for the coastal provinces.

Coastal Provinces

Guangdong's export boom and massive use of foreign capital were mainly supported by its economic integration with Hong Kong and Macao. For most coastal provinces, the existence of natural partners with both geographic proximity and mutual comparative advantages would also strongly affect their growth performance.

The Fujian Delta area has already developed strong links with Taiwan Province of China. With the latter's industry now facing skyrocketing labor and land costs, Fujian, whose unit cost of labor is still less than half that in the Pearl River Delta area, represents a highly attractive location for capital from Taiwan Province of China.[95] Trade is less dynamic than that between Guangdong and Hong Kong because of political considerations, but the potential is clearly very high.

Northeast China also has great potential, given its substantial petroleum, metallurgical, coal, chemical, and building materials industries and proximity to Japan and Korea, as well as the potential markets of Russia and the Democratic People's Republic of Korea.

The Yangtze River Delta is the home of China's most advanced industrial city, Shanghai, and two

provinces with highly market-oriented economies, Jiangsu and Zhejiang. These provinces have grown about as quickly as Guangdong even without an external partner such as Hong Kong. Foreign investment and trade associated with the opening of the Pudong New Area is likely to lead to accelerated growth in the whole delta.

There is potential in many regions of China for developing along patterns similar to, though not identical with, Guangdong's experience. It should, however, be recalled that the growth of Guangdong and other coastal provinces received a strong stimulus from investment from other parts of China that sought the benefits of a less restrictive economic environment. As economic liberalization spreads through the country, the growth should become more evenly distributed.

Conclusions

China's size has led its leadership to turn to the provinces for experiments that have stimulated reform for the past 15 years. The center has tolerated and even encouraged provincial initiatives and the widespread application of market-related reforms. These regional policies have been highly successful in generating the strong growth of some of the coastal provinces (Chart 6). Statistical analysis has

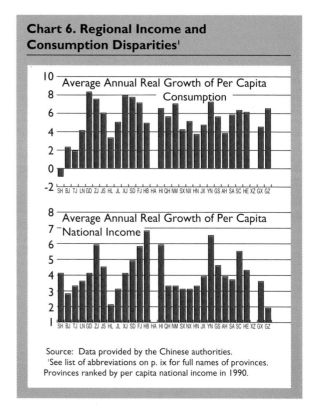

Chart 6. Regional Income and Consumption Disparities[1]

Average Annual Real Growth of Per Capita Consumption

Average Annual Real Growth of Per Capita National Income

Source: Data provided by the Chinese authorities.
[1]See list of abbreviations on p. ix for full names of provinces.
Provinces ranked by per capita national income in 1990.

---

[94]Jilin, Heilongjiang, Inner Mongolia, Xinjiang, Gansu, Tibet, Yunnan, and Guangxi. Although Liaoning borders the Democratic People's Republic of Korea, since it has a longer coastal line than a border line, it is classified here as a coastal province.

[95]See Zou, Ma, and Wang (1990).

identified some of the factors that have contributed to the rapid growth of the most successful of the coastal provinces as the extent of openness of the province; the low degree of state ownership; little government intervention in microeconomic policies; the higher amount of fiscal resources retained in the province; and the availability of foreign direct investment (see Appendix II).

However, one of the negative effects of the decentralized decision making, in the context of an underdeveloped system of indirect instruments of macroeconomic management, has been a severe weakening in macroeconomic control with adverse implications for the maintenance of macrostability. This topic is covered in more detail in the following section.

VI   Economic Impact of Reform

China's reforms were manifested in impressive output gains, particularly in agriculture, in the nonstate industrial sector and in external trade. On the negative side, the industrial sector has been retarded by the slow pace of reform in the state-owned enterprise sector. Moreover, the relatively gradual pace of reform and the inadequacy of instruments of macroeconomic control have been reflected in the recurring periods of economic instability. This section examines the effect of reforms on selected aspects of the economy. The impact of reforms is first reviewed from the perspective of the level and structure of real economic activity and the extent of China's integration into the global economy. A review is then conducted of the implications of the reforms, particularly the pronounced decentralization that has taken place, for macroeconomic management and stability. The section ends with a brief outline of the reforms necessary to enable effective market-based macroeconomic management.

Impact on Economic Activity

Growth

After the inception of the reforms, real growth accelerated markedly. Growth rates of real net material product rose from an average of about 6 percent in the 25 years between 1953 and 1978 to more than 9 percent between 1979 and 1992 (Table 1 and Chart 7). This acceleration was predominantly due to a sharp increase in the growth of total factor productivity, although increases in the growth rate of capital stock also contributed.[96] An important goal of the reform effort was to facilitate the import of technology to modernize the economy. The growth in productivity was undoubtedly reinforced by the resultant technological progress.

Agricultural Output

The agricultural sector made the most significant contribution to the increase in productivity and output growth in the early years of the reform. Between 1978 and 1984, output grew by an annual average of about 8.8 percent.[97] These impressive gains can be attributed both to the introduction of improved individual incentives embodied in the household responsibility system as well as to increases in procurement prices.[98] The growth of total agricultural production moderated to an average of about 4 percent from 1985 to 1991, reflecting a number of factors: less improvement in the relative prices of agricultural products (especially grain) than in earlier years; the resumption of the practice of requiring farmers to sell grain to the state at below-market prices; low investment in agriculture and related infrastructure by farmers, who have tended to invest in housing, and by collectives, which may have preferred to invest in TVEs; the outflow of the labor force from the cropping sector; increasing fragmentation of land holdings; and the difficulty of replicating the one-time productivity gains arising from the termination of the commune system.

Industry

The period after 1978 also witnessed more rapid growth in industrial output, but closer analysis reveals that the most significant impact came from the nonstate-owned enterprises, including TVEs, individual, and foreign-funded enterprises. The initial impact of the reforms on the state-owned enterprises was to increase the rate of growth of output from an average of 6 percent between 1980 and 1983 to over 10 percent during 1984–88. However, the SOEs did not show the same dynamism as the agricultural and

---

[96]Perkins (1988) estimates that productivity growth accounted for over 40 percent of total growth in real net material product between 1977 and 1985, whereas growth in the labor force and in the capital stock accounted for the remainder.

---

[97]The output of TVEs was included in this aggregate until 1984.

[98]Lin (1992) examines the relative importance of various components of the reform on agricultural growth in China between 1978 and 1984. He finds that the dominant source of output growth was the shift from the production team system to the household responsibility system (HRS). Changes in procurement and market prices, as well as the improved availability of fertilizers and other inputs, also had a significant impact on output growth.

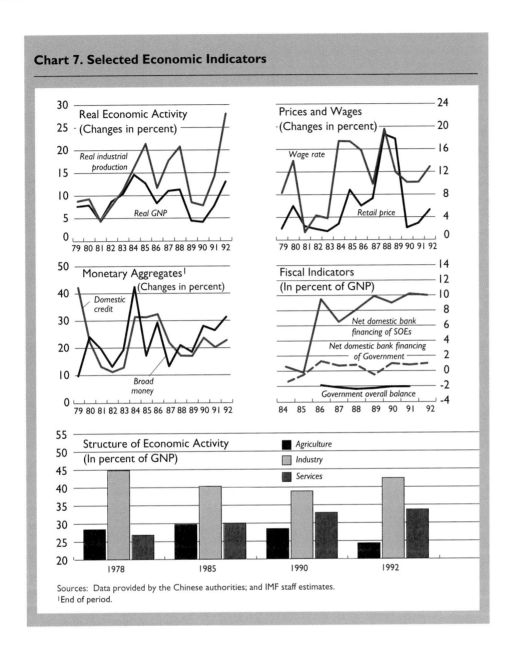

Chart 7. Selected Economic Indicators

Real Economic Activity (Changes in percent)
Real industrial production
Real GNP

Prices and Wages (Changes in percent)
Wage rate
Retail price

Monetary Aggregates[1] (Changes in percent)
Domestic credit
Broad money

Fiscal Indicators (In percent of GNP)
Net domestic bank financing of SOEs
Net domestic bank financing of Government
Government overall balance

Structure of Economic Activity (In percent of GNP)
Agriculture
Industry
Services

Sources: Data provided by the Chinese authorities; and IMF staff estimates.
[1] End of period.

nonstate-owned industrial sectors. Table 15 shows the declining share of state-owned enterprises in the gross value of industrial output from just over 80 percent in 1978 to less than 50 percent in 1992. Between 1989 and 1992, the gross value of output of the SOEs grew by an annual average of 24 percent, while that of nonstate-owned industries grew by nearly 15 percent.

The primary problem is that the objective functions of large and medium-scale state-owned enterprises are not limited to maximizing profits but include a host of other social and economic objectives. State-owned enterprises are not only a major source of employment but also perform social wel-

fare functions, such as providing housing, medical care, and education to their employees. As a result, although there is a bankruptcy law, it has been used only sparingly. The state, for its part, has protected the SOE sector through its pricing policies, the budget, and the banking system. Also, there has been little significant "hardening" of enterprise budget constraints. For the most part, the state-owned industrial sector remains characterized by overstaffed and inefficient enterprises producing goods of substandard quality, incurring losses on account of both distortions caused by pricing policies as well as fundamental inefficiency associated with the lack of competition, undertaking inappropriate investments,

Table 15. Gross Value of Industrial Output by Form of Ownership
(In percent)

	1978	1980	1985	1988	1989	1990	1991	1992
State	80.7	78.7	64.9	56.8	56.1	54.6	52.9	48.4
Collective	19.2	20.7	32.1	36.1	35.7	35.6	35.7	38.2
Of which:								
Township and village enterprises	...	...	14.6	19.5	19.6	20.2	21.0	...
Other rural and urban collectives	...	...	17.5	16.6	16.1	15.4	14.7	...
Individual	...	—	1.8	4.3	4.8	5.4	5.7	6.7
Other[1]	...	0.6	1.2	2.8	3.4	4.4	5.7	6.6

Source: *China Statistical Yearbook*, various issues.
[1]Includes foreign enterprises.

and unable to compete with the more dynamic non-state industrial sector.

The opportunities provided by the reforms in the agricultural sector for the development of "sideline" activities in the rural areas laid the foundation for rural enterprises, or township and village enterprises. Conceived as a means of absorbing surplus labor associated with rising agricultural productivity, their dynamic growth was a largely unanticipated phenomenon. It may be attributed to a number of factors, including their concentration on consumer goods that were in high demand, the ready availability of labor, the limited capital requirements, and the freedom from government controls. Moreover, no constraints were imposed by the need to overhaul existing institutions or to renew capital stock as was true for the SOEs. Finally, although the TVEs remained publicly owned (albeit at a lower level of government), they have faced a much harder budget constraint than the SOEs.

Income Distribution

The rapid growth during the first half of the 1980s led to a dramatic reduction in the incidence of poverty, from 28 percent in 1978 to less than 9 percent in 1984.[99] The large productivity and output gains in the agricultural sector resulted in a decline in rural poverty from 33 percent in 1978 to about 11 percent in 1984. Since then, however, there has been little progress on this front, despite strong growth in rural output, primarily because the once-and-for-all benefits of agricultural reforms have been reaped, and the TVEs, which are the main source of continued

growth in rural areas, have not developed in remote areas, to which poverty is now largely confined. As for the effect of reforms on income inequality, the Gini coefficient for rural households increased slightly between the early 1980s and 1990, indicating an increase in income inequality. Also, data on differential regional growth rates suggest that income disparities may have widened. However, the existence of significant interprovincial budgetary transfers may have ameliorated this development.

Integration into the Global Economy

Background

Before external sector reforms were initiated in 1978, only 12 state foreign trade corporations (FTCs), under the erstwhile Ministry of Foreign Economic Relations and Trade (MOFERT) (now known as the Ministry of Foreign Trade and Economic Cooperation—MOFTEC), were responsible for foreign trade in China. For the country as a whole, levels of exports and imports were set by the central government in the framework of government plans. The use of foreign capital in the form of borrowed resources or foreign direct investment was kept very low by design. To make foreign trade and investment more market oriented, the Government decentralized decision-making powers that affected exports and imports, as well as foreign direct investment. Areas of foreign trade subject to central planning were reduced significantly, and the Government now uses the system of import licensing and import and export duties to influence trade flows.

The Government has also used the exchange rate and the foreign exchange retention system to encourage the production of export goods. Other mea-

---

[99]See World Bank (1992a).

sures to influence China's foreign trade flows have included a reduction in the number of export commodities that are subject to quotas and to various export taxes and preferential financing for exports. To liberalize the import regime, China's tariff system has also been modified in recent years. These modifications have helped the country to reduce significantly the average level of tariff rates applied on the imports of certain goods, in particular capital goods and equipment. As a consequence, tariffs on China's industrial imports are structured so that they provide more protection to finished goods than to intermediate goods. Intermediate and capital goods are mostly subject to rates of 20–40 percent, while rates on most finished consumer goods are over 60 percent. This policy is to discourage consumption of "nonessential and luxury imports" and to provide high margins of effective protection to domestic industrial production.

China has also created a favorable environment for the use of foreign capital in recent years to accelerate the modernization of its economy. A law promulgated in 1979 defines conditions under which joint ventures can be set up in China. Tax incentives and other preferential policies are offered to foreign investors who are willing to develop projects in designated open economic zones (see Section IV above).

Trends in Foreign Trade and Investment

The policy of opening the economy to the rest of the world has resulted in a marked expansion of foreign trade and investment during the last decade. Exports in constant prices grew at an average rate of 12 percent a year in 1980–91, making China the thirteenth largest exporter in the world in 1991, up from twenty-sixth in 1980. China's merchandise trade as a ratio of its current price GNP[100] increased from 12.8 percent in 1980 to over 38 percent in 1992 (Table 16).

This increase in the relative importance of foreign trade in the Chinese economy reflected, to a large extent, the growing export orientation of the economies of coastal regions. Exports also increased rapidly with the establishment of foreign-funded enterprises. Hong Kong-based enterprises have been taking advantage of China's cheap labor and land to develop mainly labor-intensive industries in open economic zones. These enterprises have diversified China's industrial production of export goods. The share of industrial exports in China's total increased from about 50 percent in 1980 to about 80 percent in

1992. Apart from two consecutive declines in 1984–85, this ratio increased steadily during 1980–91 (Table 17).

China's industrial exports have continued to be heavily concentrated in light industrial goods. Products such as textiles, clothing, telecommunications equipment, and arts and crafts still represent a high percentage of total exports. Changes in the commodity composition of China's exports measured by the Hirschman concentration index[101] do not seem to have been significant during 1980–91. The degree of commodity concentration of China's exports declined only marginally from 41.4 percent in 1980 to slightly less than 40 percent in 1991 (Table 16).

At the same time, there has also been a relative concentration of China's foreign trade in a limited number of markets (based on China's data sources). China's direct trading partners appear to be the Asian countries that presently account for more than 65 percent of its total exports. Among these countries, Hong Kong plays a leading role. As a broad generalization, imports of intermediate and capital goods come from Asia—notably Hong Kong and Japan—and finished consumer goods are exported mainly to the United States and Europe.

Foreign capital flows have increased rapidly as a result of preferential policies offered by the Chinese Government. These policies have attracted numerous Hong Kong investors, particularly in the form of contractual joint ventures. By the end of 1992, over 80,000 foreign-funded enterprises had been approved in China. About one-third of these enterprises were in tourism and other service sectors, while the other enterprises invested in crude oil exploration and assembly and processing industries. About two-thirds of total foreign investment originated from Hong Kong. However, investment from the United States, Europe, and Japan has also increased rapidly.[102]

Assessing the Degree of Integration

In assessing the degree of China's integration into the global economy, one must take into account developments in its trade and investment flows as well as improvements in its productivity and international competitiveness. This is important because increases in China's exports[103] could result from a

---

[100]The calculation of GNP in U.S. dollars is based on the official exchange rate.

[101]This index is defined as $H = 100\sqrt{\dfrac{X_i^2}{X}}$ where X_i = exports of ith commodity and X = total exports of China.

[102]Many enterprises belong to investors in Taiwan Province of China and other countries in Southeast Asia that are listed in Hong Kong.

[103]Exports have certainly been the main objective of China's recent efforts to open its economy to the rest of the world.

Table 16. External Sector Indicators
(In billions of U.S. dollars, unless otherwise indicated)

	1980	1985	1986	1987	1988	1989	1990	1991	1992
Exports[1]	18.1	27.3	30.9	39.4	47.5	52.5	62.1	71.9	85.0
Imports[1]	20.0	42.3	42.9	43.2	55.3	59.2	53.4	63.8	80.6
Exports (1980 prices)[1]	18.2	31.6	36.3	41.4	47.0	50.6	55.4	63.9	73.2
Imports (1980 prices)[1]	20.0	44.8	39.5	37.5	44.9	49.7	42.5	50.0	61.8
Imports to GNP ratio	6.7	14.5	15.3	14.2	14.7	14.0	14.4	17.1	18.8
Exports to GNP ratio	6.1	9.4	11.0	12.9	12.6	12.4	16.8	19.3	19.8
Openness of economy	12.8	23.9	26.3	27.1	27.3	26.4	31.2	36.4	38.6
Real growth rate of exports		9.8	15.2	14.1	13.5	7.6	9.4	15.3	14.7
Real growth rate of imports		53.4	−11.8	−5.1	19.7	10.7	−14.6	17.8	23.6
China's share of world exports	1.0	1.5	1.6	1.7	1.8	1.8	1.9	2.1	2.1
China's share of world imports	1.0	2.2	2.1	1.8	2.0	2.0	1.6	1.8	2.0
China's share of world trade	1.0	1.9	1.8	1.7	1.9	1.9	1.7	1.9	2.0
Commodity concentration coefficient for exports	41.4	39.9	38.4	38.6	38.7	38.6	38.9	40.0	...
Commodity concentration coefficient for imports	42.9	50.1	49.5	45.1	42.9	42.8	42.9	42.9	...
Memorandum items:									
GNP (*in billions of yuan*)	447.0	855.8	969.6	1,135.1	1,401.5	1,591.6	1,769.5	1,985.5	2,362.8
Official exchange rate (*RMB per U.S. dollar*)	1.498	1.937	1.453	3.722	3.722	3.765	4.783	5.323	5.515
GNP (*in billions of U.S. dollars*)	298.4	291.4	280.8	305.0	376.5	422.7	369.9	373.0	428.4

Sources: China Customs Statistics, various issues; *China Statistical Yearbook*, various issues; and IMF staff estimates.
[1]On a customs basis.

reduction in domestic absorption of some of its export commodities or an increase in the utilization of previously idle production capacity. In these two cases, China's exports could increase even when its productivity and international competitiveness have not improved. Such an expansion of exports would be transient because it could end as soon as all existing capacity has been utilized or domestic absorption of exportable goods can no longer be reduced.

Various indicators, including changes in labor productivity and the behavior of China's real effective exchange rate (Charts 8 and 9), point to productivity increases and inexpensive labor as important factors in the rapid growth of exports. As a result, the country's share of world trade almost doubled, from 1 percent in 1980 to 1.9 percent in 1991. At the same time, its share of world imports increased from 1 percent in 1980 to 1.8 percent in 1991 (Chart 10). China's GNP also became more dependent on export production during that period. From 6.1 percent of GNP in 1980, the ratio of China's exports to GNP rose to 19.3 percent in 1991 (Chart 11).[104]

The heavy concentration of China's foreign trade in terms of its commodity composition and trading partner countries suggests that China still has considerable potential to increase its relative weight in world trade. The Hirschman commodity concentration indices for China's foreign trade during 1980–

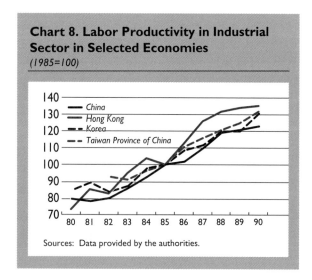

Chart 8. Labor Productivity in Industrial Sector in Selected Economies
(1985=100)

Sources: Data provided by the authorities.

---

[104]These ratios tend to overstate the degree of openness of the Chinese economy because they are based on the official exchange rate of the domestic currency.

Table 17. Foreign Trade by Major Commodity Groups
(In percent of total)

	1980	1985	1986	1987	1988	1989	1990	1991	1992
Exports	100.0	100.0	100.0	100.0	100.0	100.0	100.0	100.0	100.0
Primary products	50.3	50.5	36.4	33.5	30.3	28.7	25.6	22.5	20.1
Foodstuffs	16.4	13.9	14.4	12.1	12.4	11.7	10.6	10.1	9.8
Beverages	0.4	0.4	0.4	0.4	0.5	0.6	0.5	0.8	...
Nonfood items	9.4	9.7	9.4	9.3	8.9	8.0	5.7	4.9	3.7
Mineral fuels	23.6	26.1	11.9	11.5	8.3	8.2	8.4	6.6	5.5
Of which: crude oil	...	24.8	10.4	10.1	7.4	6.9	7.2	5.5	...
Animal and vegetable oils and fats	0.3	0.5	0.4	0.2	0.1	0.2	0.3	0.2	...
Industrial products	49.7	49.5	63.6	66.5	69.7	71.3	74.4	77.5	79.9
Chemicals	6.2	5.0	5.6	5.7	6.1	6.1	6.0	5.3	5.1
Products classified by material	22.1	16.4	19.0	21.7	22.1	20.8	20.3	20.1	19.0
Of which: textiles	...	11.9	13.7	14.7	13.6	13.3	11.3	10.8	...
Machinery and equipment	4.6	2.8	3.5	4.4	5.8	7.4	9.0	10.0	15.6
Miscellaneous manufactures	15.7	12.8	16.0	15.9	17.4	20.5	20.4	23.1	22.1
Of which: clothing	...	7.5	9.5	9.5	10.3	11.7	11.0	12.5	...
Unclassified items	1.2	12.5	19.4	18.7	18.3	16.6	18.7	19.0	18.2
Imports	100.0	100.0	100.0	100.0	100.0	100.0	100.0	100.0	...
Primary products	34.8	12.5	13.1	16.0	18.2	19.9	18.5	17.0	...
Foodstuffs	14.6	3.7	3.8	5.6	6.3	7.1	6.3	4.4	...
Beverages and tobacco	0.2	0.5	0.4	0.6	0.6	0.3	0.3	0.3	...
Nonfood items	17.7	7.7	7.3	7.7	9.2	8.2	7.7	7.8	...
Mineral fuels	1.0	0.4	1.2	1.2	1.4	2.8	2.4	3.3	...
Animal and vegetable oils and fats	1.2	0.3	0.5	0.8	0.7	1.5	1.8	1.1	...
Industrial products	65.2	87.5	86.9	84.0	81.8	80.1	81.5	83.0	...
Chemicals	14.5	10.6	8.8	11.6	16.5	12.8	12.5	14.5	...
Products classified by material									
Of which: textiles	20.7	28.2	26.1	22.5	18.8	20.9	16.7	16.4	...
Machinery and equipment	25.6	38.4	39.1	33.8	30.2	30.8	31.6	30.7	...
Miscellaneous manufactures									
Of which: clothing	2.7	4.5	4.4	4.3	3.6	3.5	3.9	3.8	...
Unclassified items	1.6	5.8	8.5	11.8	12.6	12.2	16.9	17.5	...

Sources: China Customs Statistics; and IMF staff estimates.

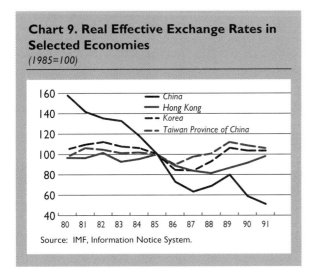

Chart 9. Real Effective Exchange Rates in Selected Economies
(1985=100)

— China
— Hong Kong
-- Korea
-- Taiwan Province of China

Source: IMF, Information Notice System.

91 clearly show that there has been a small diversification of the country's export base. For the same period, the concentration of imports did not change, although the concentration index fell during 1985–91 because of increased operations of foreign-funded enterprises during that period.

In addition to policies to promote exports and attract foreign direct investment in China, the authorities adopted measures to facilitate other financial flows between China and the rest of the world. Enterprises from mainland China began to raise capital on the Hong Kong stock market during the late 1980s, and the amount of bonds issued by Chinese agencies in various external markets increased substantially between 1980 and 1986. Although this amount fell between 1987 and 1991, it began to pick up again in 1992. Reflecting this issuance of bonds and the use of other forms of foreign borrowing,

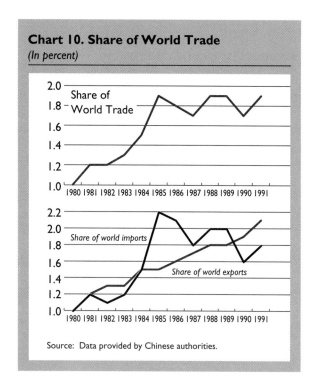

Chart 10. Share of World Trade
(In percent)

Source: Data provided by Chinese authorities.

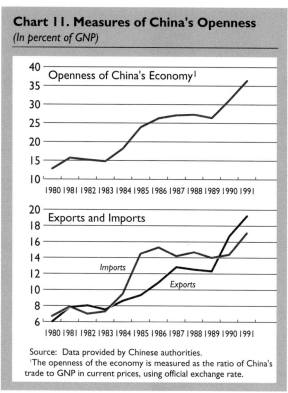

Chart 11. Measures of China's Openness
(In percent of GNP)

Source: Data provided by Chinese authorities.
[1]The openness of the economy is measured as the ratio of China's trade to GNP in current prices, using official exchange rate.

China's external debt is estimated to have increased rapidly during 1980–92. Public and publicly guaranteed debt increased from $4.5 billion in 1980 to over $58 billion in 1992, of which total outstanding debt borrowed from commercial banks increased from $1.5 billion in 1980 to about $18 billion in 1992. As a result, outstanding external debt as a ratio of exports of goods and nonfactor services increased more than threefold, from 22.4 percent in 1980 to 78.4 percent in 1992. Investments in equity shares are also increasingly taking place between China and the rest of the world. China is actively supporting the sale of special shares to foreigners at the stock exchange markets in Shanghai and Shenzhen.

A further indicator of the increasing significance of China in the global economy is the rise in its share of the international (non-gold) reserves of reporting territories. From less than 1 percent in 1978, China's reserves increased—notably in the later years of the period—to about 5 percent at end-1991. In absolute terms, its ranking rose from fortieth to seventh during this period.

In conclusion, measured in terms of trade and investment flows, China's economy has become increasingly integrated into the world economy. One manifestation of this integration is the narrowing of the gap between domestic and international prices of many tradable goods as a result of price reforms. This process will be strengthened by the recent opening of the service sector and the inland prov-

inces to foreign trade and investment and the intention to adopt international conventions and practices in accounting and in the legal and regulatory framework.

Decentralization and Macroeconomic Policy

Section V reviewed center-local relations in the fiscal, financial, and external areas. An examination of the various institutions suggests that, although decision making has been extensively decentralized, many aspects of the planning process are replicated at the provincial level, which has retarded efforts to develop an indirect system of macroeconomic management.

Fiscal Policy

In the fiscal area, the ad hoc nature of the contractual relations between the central and local governments has led to a tendency for overall expenditures to exceed the approved budget. Since local governments are generally not permitted to run deficits,[105] Wong (1991) points out that there have been three

---

[105]As an exception, Shanghai was authorized in 1992 to issue bonds for the specific purpose of developing the Pudong New Area.

types of responses to local demand pressures: first, local authorities have attempted to negotiate more favorable fiscal packages with the center; second, they have stepped outside the normal budgetary process by tapping the very large "extrabudgetary funds" of locally owned SOEs; third, they have attempted to expand the local tax base by promoting local economic growth. To these may be added a fourth development that has become increasingly common in the 1990s: the various means of circumventing the prohibition on the issue of bonds or bank borrowing. For instance, in 1992–93, it is reported that many local authorities and SOEs issued various forms of financial instruments.[106]

These different responses have together imparted an expansionary bias to fiscal policy as they have led to overall expenditures financed directly or indirectly through borrowing. Moreover, the risk of inefficient duplication of investment is heightened as provinces finance their investment with extrabudgetary funds generated from enterprises under their jurisdiction. The significance of the extrabudgetary funds is illustrated in Table 13. The secular decline in the government revenue/GNP ratio was offset by the growth of extrabudgetary funds through the mid-1980s, although subsequently the latter also began to decline. Cross-provincial data for 1990 further illustrate the significance of the extrabudgetary funds when considered together with budgetary resources (Chart 4), although it would appear that the overall level of extrabudgetary operations does not alter the financial balance in most provinces. It must be stressed that the bulk of the resources in the extrabudgetary funds are enterprises' funds that are not automatically at the disposal of governments but represent an additional revenue base—equivalent to 5–18 percent of GNP across the provinces—that local governments may attempt to tap.

Also, as local governments have been allowed to make direct investments in industry or commerce and have done so to increase local revenues to cover local expenditures, it may be argued that it was the imperative of raising revenue that spurred the growth observed in many provinces. Clearly this has been one way in which signals concerning reforms emanating from the center are quickly translated into growth. It has also been a source of macroeconomic pressure: since local expenditure is not regulated within a coherent overall economic framework, there is a greater risk of overheating, particularly where local governments bring pressure to bear on banks for additional lending or issue bonds without authorization.

Monetary Policy

As with fiscal policy, in credit policy provincial authorities may pursue local objectives that are not consistent with national policies, bringing pressure to bear on the provincial banking system that undermines the center's monetary policy goals. With the establishment of a two-tiered banking system, various instruments have acquired greater significance in the conduct of monetary policy, including lending to banks by the People's Bank, reserve requirements, and—to an increasing extent—interest rates. However, the credit plan remains the principal instrument of monetary policy. Although it is formulated at the national level in accordance with macroeconomic targets of real growth and inflation, its implementation is highly decentralized; as a consequence the annual credit ceiling has generally been exceeded.

Until 1988, monitoring and control of the credit plan was relatively lax. In 1989, under the rectification program, it was tightened, with considerable powers being retrieved by the center. The subsequent relaxation of the monetary policy stance has been accompanied by a corresponding relaxation of control over the credit plan. In 1991, limited autonomy was given to the provincial branches to make small variations in the composition of credit expansion under the plan. In 1992 and 1993 there have been growing signs of pressure for greater autonomy in credit allocation. Indeed, against the background of local pressure for investment funds, the banks have extended credit by means outside the normal credit plan.

External Policies

The authorities' strategy of moving toward a unified market-oriented exchange rate is hampered by local restrictions on the free flow of foreign exchange and the absence of an integrated national market. In this environment, there is no guarantee of uniform conditions for access to the market, since access is determined at the local level by the branches of the SAEC. Furthermore, evidence suggests that the restrictiveness of the trade regime varies widely among provinces and regions in China.

Macroeconomic Management and Stability[107]

Background

Since 1978, China has experienced periods of macroeconomic instability that have interacted with

---

[106]These local bonds have been in use for some years, albeit on a relatively limited level. They have sometimes been used to finance infrastructure. Many local enterprises have also issued their own bonds.

[107]This section draws on Khor (1991).

Table 18. Selected Macroeconomic Indicators
(Annual percent change, unless otherwise specified)

	1980	1981	1982	1983	1984	1985	1986	1987	1988	1989	1990	1991	1992
Real GNP	7.9	4.4	8.8	10.4	14.7	12.8	8.1	10.9	11.3	4.4	4.1	7.7	13.0
Real gross industrial output	9.3	4.3	7.8	11.2	16.3	21.4	11.7	17.7	20.8	8.5	7.8	14.5	22.0
Real gross fixed investment	2.9	−12.5	28.0	14.7	22.7	27.3	13.3	14.7	10.4	−15.5	1.2	18.8	28.2
Retail prices													
Period average	6.0	2.4	1.9	1.5	2.8	8.8	6.0	7.3	18.6	17.8	2.1	2.9	5.3
End of period	22.2	2.6	0.1	3.7	4.8	10.7	6.2	9.1	26.7	6.4	2.2	4.0	6.7
Broad money	24.1	19.7	13.1	19.2	42.4	17.1	29.3	13.2	21.0	18.4	28.0	26.4	31.3
Domestic credit	22.3	13.1	11.2	12.8	31.4	31.3	34.1	22.3	18.9	17.1	23.7	20.2	22.8
Net domestic assets	...	...	...	...	...	...	33.9	21.5	20.7	18.3	24.1	25.0	32.7
Merchandise exports[1]	33.7	20.5	−4.0	−2.0	15.4	5.0	2.6	34.9	18.2	5.3	19.2	17.8	18.6
Merchandise imports[1]	24.8	12.6	−16.4	−10.9	27.6	60.0	−8.7	4.3	27.4	5.3	−13.3	22.3	26.2
Trade balance (*in billions of U.S. dollars*)	−1.9	—	3.0	0.8	−1.3	−14.8	−12.0	−3.8	−7.7	−6.6	8.7	8.1	4.4
							(In percent of GNP)						
Current account balance	0.3	0.9	2.1	1.5	0.8	−4.0	−2.6	0.1	−1.0	−1.0	3.2	3.6	1.5
Overall budgetary balance	−3.3	−1.3	−1.4	−1.7	−1.5	−0.5	−2.0	−2.2	−2.4	−2.4	−2.1	−2.5	−2.5
Revenue	29.4	29.0	27.2	27.4	26.4	26.6	25.1	22.8	20.0	20.5	19.9	18.4	17.0
Expenditure	32.7	30.3	28.6	29.1	27.9	27.1	27.1	25.0	22.4	22.9	22.0	20.9	19.5

Sources: *China Statistical Yearbook*, 1992; and data provided by the Chinese authorities.
[1]In U.S. dollar terms.

the implementation of reform. Macroeconomic cycles are not unique to China or to the post-reform period, although their characteristics have been altered by the advent of reform. In the pre-reform period, owing to pervasive price and trade controls, the cycles were manifested in wide swings in the growth of output. In the post-reform period, not unexpectedly, the cyclical episodes have been characterized by fluctuations in the inflation rate and the balance of payments, with less pronounced swings in output growth. Although it is difficult to assess which type of instability imposes higher costs on the economy, the Chinese authorities, perhaps as a consequence of the hyperinflationary experience of the late 1940s, attach great importance to price stability. Their concern that too rapid a pace of reform might exacerbate inflation is heightened by their desire to avoid a repetition of the social turbulence of earlier years.

The macroeconomic cycles have had a number of characteristics in common: an increase in aggregate demand, especially investment demand associated with an acceleration or new phase of reform; the ratification of the increase in aggregate demand through credit expansion, reflecting the tendency by economic agents to equate the acceleration of reforms with a call for higher growth; the emergence

of shortages and bottlenecks in critical sectors that led to an acceleration in inflation and/or a deterioration of the balance of payments—"overheating"; and finally, attempts to stabilize the economy primarily through the imposition of administrative controls and a slowdown, or, in some cases, a partial reversal, of the reform process.[108]

The Cycles

First Cycle: 1979–82

During this first cycle, agricultural reform was initiated, and profit retention by enterprises replaced profit transfers to the state. The resultant increase in rural incomes, as well as the worsening of the overall fiscal balance (the latter owing both to a decline in revenues and to a sharp increase in subsidies as higher agricultural procurement prices were not passed on to consumers), led to a surge in aggregate demand. At the same time, domestic investment growth also rose sharply (Table 18). Credit ex-

---

[108]In two of the cycles in which external imbalances were pronounced, China made use of IMF resources (first credit tranche stand-by arrangements in 1981 and 1986).

panded rapidly to accommodate the demand growth; the seasonally adjusted annualized quarterly growth rate rose from 12.5 percent in mid-1979 to 25 percent by the end of 1979 and remained high throughout 1980 (Table 19 and Chart 12). Inflation accelerated to nearly 20 percent on an annualized basis in the fourth quarter of 1979 and the trade balance deteriorated sharply. The authorities responded by tightening some price controls in 1980, direct credit controls and trade policies during 1981, and slashing the state's investment budget. Inflation fell, output growth moderated, and, with a short lag, import growth was compressed and the trade balance swung into surplus by the third quarter of 1981.

Second Cycle: 1984–Early 1986

Beginning in 1984, the two-tier pricing system was introduced, enterprises were granted greater autonomy in setting wages, a two-tier banking system was established, and a phased liberalization of the foreign trade regime was initiated. Again, aggregate demand grew sharply as enterprises, subject to their customary soft budget constraints, granted large increases in wages and increased their investment spending. At the same time, the People's Bank of China had not been vested with the operational or institutional instruments necessary to control credit expansion effectively in the new, more decentralized banking system. Credit expansion rose from an annualized rate of 9 percent in the first quarter to 76 percent by the fourth quarter of 1984. The decentralization of foreign trade decisions led to a spillover of excess demand into the balance of payments. By mid-1985, inflation and import growth had accelerated sharply. Once again, the authorities responded by tightening credit, foreign trade, and exchange controls. In addition, interest rates were increased and the renminbi devalued.

Third Cycle: Mid-1986–Late 1988

In this period the contract responsibility system for enterprises was introduced, restrictions on the operations of specialized banks were lowered, and universal banks and the first FEACs were established. Largely reflecting a sharp deterioration in the overall budgetary balance, aggregate demand growth accelerated. The increases in several administered prices in early 1988 were implemented in an already overheated economy and exacerbated existing inflationary expectations; the quarterly inflation rate soared from an annual rate of 14 percent in the first quarter of 1988 to 21 percent in the second quarter and reached an alarming 43 percent in the third quarter. The authorities' response was a

system-wide retrenchment that began in late 1988— the rectification program—under which administrative controls on imports and credit were tightened, some price controls were recentralized, and state investment expenditure was slashed. During 1989, interest rates were increased, and the renminbi was devalued by 21 percent. Inflation and the growth rates of industrial production and imports slowed, and the external balance turned sharply into surplus.

The most recent retrenchment was particularly pronounced because it was associated with renewed debate within the leadership about China's reform process. Fundamental questions were raised, including considerations of ownership and even broader political issues. Following a hiatus of almost three years, the pace of reform began to regain momentum during 1991.

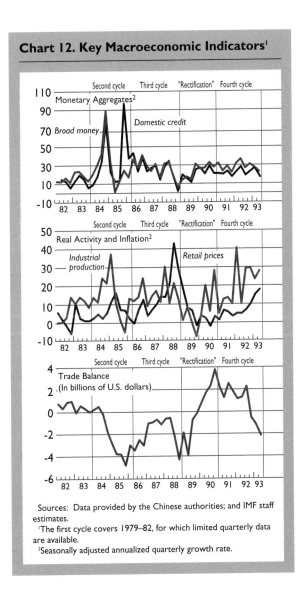

Chart 12. Key Macroeconomic Indicators[1]

Sources: Data provided by the Chinese authorities; and IMF staff estimates.
[1]The first cycle covers 1979–82, for which limited quarterly data are available.
[2]Seasonally adjusted annualized quarterly growth rate.

Table 19. Key Macroeconomic Indicators
(Seasonally adjusted annualized quarterly rates, unless otherwise indicated)

	Industrial Production	Domestic Credit	Retail Price Index	Import Growth[1]	Trade Balance[2]
1980 I	...	21.1	10.9	...	...
II	4.5	25.2	2.6	...	...
III	6.4	21.9	3.1	...	...
IV	−13.8	21.3	1.2	...	...
1981 I	3.4	12.0	3.1	...	−1.5
II	10.8	11.7	1.7	−1.6	−1.1
III	14.8	15.8	3.8	−63.8	1.0
IV	21.0	13.4	1.2	−18.6	1.4
1982 I	0.2	12.8	5.7	14.3	0.8
II	0.4	14.8	1.9	33.1	0.3
III	2.9	12.5	−1.7	−28.4	0.9
IV	14.4	5.6	−5.8	−13.7	1.0
1983 I	10.3	12.7	10.4	39.8	−0.1
II	13.9	19.4	2.5	5.5	0.6
III	11.9	14.9	1.2	71.7	0.3
IV	8.9	5.6	1.2	6.4	—
1984 I	13.5	8.9	2.6	3.6	0.3
II	11.1	17.7	4.7	5.4	0.5
III	24.2	34.1	2.4	68.7	−0.2
IV	22.1	76.1	5.3	46.5	−1.8
1985 I	36.8	−3.3	11.6	163.9	−2.8
II	11.1	45.9	16.1	41.3	−3.8
III	1.4	15.5	7.0	31.7	−3.8
IV	−4.6	25.2	6.7	22.8	−4.8
1986 I	12.7	25.0	2.1	−37.3	−3.0
II	11.8	30.2	−0.4	50.7	−3.5
III	13.9	29.1	7.2	−18.2	−2.5
IV	24.8	48.1	12.4	−9.8	−3.0
1987 I	8.9	22.4	3.7	−19.0	−1.0
II	14.2	22.4	7.0	18.4	−1.0
III	16.9	27.4	9.7	13.0	−0.7
IV	11.9	18.0	14.1	43.5	−1.2
1988 I	29.9	27.0	13.7	1.6	−0.6
II	10.5	24.9	21.3	33.8	−0.6
III	20.8	19.9	42.8	57.3	−2.5
IV	13.7	0.8	28.7	48.0	−4.3
1989 I	1.0	19.3	18.1	−25.3	−1.9
II	7.9	14.2	7.8	59.9	−3.9
III	−0.2	11.1	6.6	−36.4	−0.7
IV	−6.4	26.0	−1.8	−37.2	−0.1
1990 I	−3.7	26.8	3.6	−9.2	−0.7
II	27.4	20.2	3.4	6.3	1.7
III	5.2	28.5	2.8	12.8	2.3
IV	31.4	20.8	3.0	22.4	3.8
1991 I	−4.2	21.3	1.3	8.7	2.2
II	22.2	19.4	7.6	37.4	1.3
III	12.1	23.1	5.2	25.0	2.5
IV	13.5	17.9	3.0	2.4	1.8
1992 I	25.9	23.0	4.5	20.6	1.2
II	21.5	28.9	6.0	44.9	1.3
III	27.0	17.8	6.3	8.6	2.5
IV	33.3	22.1	9.8	80.0	−0.7
1993 I	11.7	20.6	14.7	−17.0	−1.2
II	40.5	...	15.0	41.4	−3.6

Sources: IMF, *International Financial Statistics*, various issues; and data provided by the Chinese authorities.
[1] In U.S. dollar terms.
[2] In billions of U.S. dollars.

Fourth Cycle: Late 1991–Present

A new phase in the process of opening and reforming the Chinese economy began in 1992. The process of opening the economy was extended, which had previously been largely confined to specific enclaves in coastal areas and other special economic zones, to encompass several inland and border areas, and far-reaching price reforms were implemented. Prices of commodities that were hitherto considered "off-limits," such as the urban ration prices of grain and various energy products, were adjusted. More recently, grain prices have been completely liberalized in several provinces. In addition to rationalizing the price system, some steps were taken to increase the exposure of the SOEs to the market and to make them responsible for their profits and losses.

The acceleration of reforms once again fueled an investment boom that by and large was accommodated by expansionary domestic financial policies. The growth of fixed investment reached 24 percent in 1992 in real terms and accelerated further, to about 40 percent, in the first half of 1993. Credit growth exceeded the plan target, and credit creation by nonbank financial intermediaries not covered by the credit plan grew rapidly, as evidenced by the increasing divergence between the growth rates of domestic credit and net domestic assets.

Signs that the economy was being stretched to its limits began to emerge during 1992 in the form of shortages in critical areas such as transportation, energy, and industrial raw materials. Inflation accelerated, especially during the first half of 1993, when the 12–month rate of change in the national retail price index was over 10 percent, and the urban cost of living index surged to almost 20 percent (Table 20). At the same time, import growth topped 25 percent, and export growth progressively slowed to below 10 percent as goods were diverted toward domestic markets.

Consequently, a deficit emerged in the trade account for the first time since 1989. Pressure in the foreign exchange market manifested itself both in the loss of official foreign exchange reserves relative to their peak in mid-1992 and in the sharp depreciation of the renminbi in swap markets by nearly 75 percent between April 1992 and June 1993. Signs of growing financial disintermediation also emerged as shown by declines in household savings deposits and the surge in demand for gold and real estate.

Amid deepening concern about the intensification of demand pressures, the authorities implemented small increases in interest rates on deposits and loans in May and again in July 1993. Other measures that were announced as part of the austerity program included reducing government expenditure by 20 percent, postponing price reforms planned for the second half of the year, limiting the number of permitted development zones, strengthening the central bank to ensure that the credit plan was adhered to and to limit credit expansion through nonbank financial intermediaries, eliminating the issuance of IOUs to farmers, strengthening the enforcement of capital gains taxes on real estate transactions, requiring loans for speculative real estate purchases to be repaid, and completing government bond sales through compulsory placement with state employees. It remains to be seen whether these measures will be sufficient to deal with the overheating, to ensure that the Chinese economy will achieve a "soft landing," and that the pace of reform will not be adversely affected.

Understanding the Cycles

At each stage in the reform process, measures emphasizing decentralization and devolution of powers and diminishing the role of the plan were followed by a surge in aggregate demand—reflecting feverish investment growth and wage increases. In general, acceleration in the reform process has been taken as a *carte blanche* for more rapid investment both by the state and nonstate sector.

At the same time, market-based macroeconomic management has been hampered by the incompleteness of the reforms. The issue here is not so much that there is a paucity of market-based policy instruments but rather that the mechanisms by which changes in these policy instruments are transmitted to real economic activity—interest rates, relative commodity prices, and exchange rates—do not always reflect underlying demand and supply conditions. Furthermore, many economic agents are not subject to the discipline of the market and therefore cannot respond to the price signals as much as would be expected in a fully market-based system. This, together with the lack of adequate legal and regulatory institutional infrastructure, has led the authorities to resort to administrative measures to control the pace of economic activity.

In addition, the implementation of some aspects of the reforms, notably of the tax system, have led to perverse automatic stabilizers. For example, the introduction of the contract responsibility system resulted in a reduction in the income elasticity of the tax system. In theory, under the contract responsibility system, profits up to the predetermined quota are taxed at a flat rate; profits above this limit are taxed at much lower rates. However, most enterprise income tax payments took the form of negotiated contracts specifying tax payments in nominal terms. To soften the impact of increased borrowing to finance

Table 20. Selected Recent Economic Indicators
(Percentage change over 12 months, unless otherwise specified)

	1990	1991	1992				1993				
			Mar.	June	Sept.	Dec.	Mar.	Apr.	May	June	July
Economic activity											
Real GNP[1]	4.5	7.7	...	...	...	13.0	15.0[2]	...	...	13.9[3]	...
Industrial production	14.5	7.8	20.1	19.6	20.7	32.2	18.3	25.0	27.3	30.2	25.1
Prices											
Retail price index	2.2	4.0	5.0	4.1	5.7	6.7	10.2	10.9	12.5	13.9	...
Cost of living index (in 35 major cities)	5.4	7.6	10.9	8.2	12.3	13.3	15.7	17.0	19.5	21.6	23.9
Monetary aggregates											
Currency in circulation	12.8	20.2	20.6	25.4	30.3	36.4	46.2	...	...	54.2	...
Broad money	28.0	26.4	26.8	29.7	29.1	31.3	30.3	...	...	26.6	...
Domestic credit	23.7	20.2	20.9	23.1	21.8	22.8	22.3	...	...	20.0	...
Net domestic assets	24.1	25.0	26.8	30.3	30.1	32.7	33.5	...	...	30.0	...
Interest rates *(in percent)*											
One-year individual deposits	8.64	7.56	7.56	7.56	7.56	7.56	7.56	7.56	9.18[4]	11.0[5]	11.0
On state industrial and commercial loans	9.36	8.64	8.64	8.64	8.64	8.64	8.64	8.64	9.36[3,6]	10.7[6]	10.7
External trade (cumulative, customs basis)											
Exports	18.3	15.3	11.9	15.2	17.0	18.7	7.5	7.4	7.7	4.3	4.7
Imports	−8.6	18.3	24.3	23.0	21.2	26.1	25.4	24.7	26.9	23.1	25.8
Trade balance *(in billions of U.S. dollars)*	8.1	7.7	1.2	2.5	5.3	4.4	−1.2	−1.9	−3.2	−3.6	−4.7
International reserves *(in billions of U.S. dollars)*											
Total	30.2	44.3	45.1	46.8	46.9	46.8	...	...	...	...	...
State foreign exchange reserves	13.1	23.3	...	...	23.2	19.4	19.8	19.6	19.5	18.9	...
Exchange rates											
Official exchange rate (Y/$)	5.2	5.4	5.5	5.5	5.5	5.7	5.7	5.7	5.8	5.8	5.8
Swap market exchange rate (Y/$)	5.7	5.9	6.0	6.4	6.6	7.3	9.0	9.7	10.1	9.7	8.8
Spread *(in percent)*	9.6	9.3	9.1	16.4	20.0	28.1	57.9	70.2	74.1	67.8	51.7

Sources: State Statistical Bureau newsletter, various issues; and data provided by the Chinese authorities.
[1] Change for whole year.
[2] Change in first quarter of 1993.
[3] Change in first half of 1993.
[4] Effective mid-May 1993.
[5] Effective July 10, 1993.
[6] For lending of one year's maturity.

enterprise investment, amortization payments were made tax deductible.

Under these arrangements, as output and profits expand, enterprises tend to retain a larger portion of their profits, which leads to an income elasticity of less than unity for the enterprise profit tax. Similarly, so long as enterprises continue to face soft budget constraints, and the tax system is not broadened and rationalized, fiscal policy will have to continue to rely on expenditure cuts to control aggregate demand. Incomplete price reform and the resultant subsidies to consumers and enterprises have implied

that expenditure cuts have to be concentrated in investment outlays with deleterious consequences for basic infrastructure.

Why should one be concerned with these bouts of macroeconomic instability when China has managed to sustain high growth rates throughout the period since reform began? The impact of "stop-go" reforms on production and resource allocation is disguised by measured growth rates, which, albeit fluctuating, remained positive even in the trough of the cycles. First, growth rates were artificially sustained in recession to protect employment through preferential credit policies. Second, measured growth rates did not reflect the continued production of large quantities of substandard and unmarketable goods by state-owned enterprises, which gave rise to interenterprise arrears and nonperforming assets in banks' portfolios. Third, in light of frequent changes in the direction of policy, investment decisions tended to be based on short-term considerations, with potentially adverse implications for the efficiency of resource allocation. Fourth, without market-based instruments of macroeconomic management, the authorities relied on direct credit controls that do not distinguish between more and less efficient borrowers. Inefficiencies in resource allocation were further aggravated as some loss-making state enterprises were supported through preferential credit. The sharp contraction in the growth of output and employment in the TVE sector during the rectification program of 1988–89 was a good example.

Structural Reforms to Promote Market-Based Macromanagement

China's experience with periodic bouts of inflation and external payments disequilibria during the implementation of reform leads to two generalizations. First, incomplete reforms heighten the risk of macroeconomic imbalances emerging. Reforms must therefore be as comprehensive as possible and must include at an early stage the development of indirect instruments with which to regulate the economy. Second, the instability stems not so much from too rapid a pace of reform but rather from excessive demand growth as new reforms are initiated. This suggests that, inasmuch as reforms do proceed in stages, new phases of reform should be accompanied by appropriately tight financial policies.

The critical issue now involves the steps that China must take to develop the capability to manage its economy through indirect means. This need has been made more acute because as economic reforms have deepened and decentralization has accelerated, administrative controls are becoming less effective leaving the authorities no choice but to rely on more market-based instruments for macroeconomic control. However, such instruments cannot work as intended without certain critical enabling structural reforms in the sectors discussed below (many of which are already being actively considered by China's policymakers and are covered in detail in Section III).

Financial Sector

The steps that would be essential to improving the functioning of financial markets are, first, strength-

ened competition in the banking sector, inter alia, by reducing the degree of specialization among the major banks and allowing them greater flexibility in setting their lending and deposit rates; second, measures should be implemented to facilitate the growth of well-functioning financial markets for interbank transactions and for short-term bills, and an appropriate legal and regulatory framework should be established. The key to successful reform in this area would be to free the specialized banks from the obligations to undertake "policy lending," or, more generally, quasi-fiscal operations at the behest of the Government in support of specific policies, sectors, or enterprises.

For a time, while the groundwork is being laid for the development of indirect instruments, it will undoubtedly be necessary for the authorities to use a combination of both direct and indirect instruments. Even so, available direct instruments can be altered somewhat to minimize their distortionary effects and increase their effectiveness. During the transitional period when it is necessary to rely on the credit plan, key steps would be (1) to expand the coverage of the credit plan to include credit to the Government;[109] (2) to begin phasing out the industry- and sector-specific allocative guidelines within the overall credit plan; and (3) to strengthen the institutional capacity of the People's Bank to implement the credit plan by enhancing headquarters control over its provincial branches.

Enterprise Reform

Market-based instruments of monetary and fiscal policy will only be effective if enterprises are subject to the discipline of the market. Enterprise reform should therefore focus on eliminating, as quickly as possible, the two key sources of operating losses by reducing, first, price distortions arising from continued price controls, and second, the inefficiency of individual enterprises associated, inter alia, with a soft budget constraint.

The first involves accelerating further the time frame for price adjustments of energy products and transportation, as the majority of SOE losses are concentrated in these sectors. For the second, the approach should be to harden SOEs' budget constraints while granting them greater autonomy. This approach would entail encouraging banks to deny credit to uncreditworthy clients and phasing out subsidies for loss-making SOEs. In addition, the au-

---

[109]The effectiveness of the credit plan, in its present form, has been greatly diminished by both the growing disintermediation and the rising amount of credit being created by NBFIs outside the credit plan.

thorities would need to accept some enterprise closures and labor force retrenchment as an outcome of these reforms. In this context, providing an adequate social safety net and creating conditions conducive to greater labor mobility—notably by establishing arrangements for pensions, health insurance, housing, and so forth, which are independent of individual work units—are crucial.

Fiscal Reform

To strengthen the role of the budget in macroeconomic management, it is necessary to tackle the problems of the lack of revenue buoyancy, the erosion in the central government's share of fiscal revenue, and the high subsidy payments. First, it will be necessary to abandon the contract system of taxation and move to a uniform enterprise income tax. Not only would this broaden the tax base and increase the elasticity of the tax system but it would also ensure that the tax system functions as an automatic stabilizer. The introduction of other direct and indirect taxes would also contribute. Second, the current revenue-sharing contracts with the provinces need to be replaced through the clearer delineation of revenue sources for central and local governments. Third, further significant price reforms, particularly

in the area of energy and transportation pricing, will need to be implemented to reduce the burden of subsidies on the budget.

External Sector Policies

A more open and liberal trade and exchange system would provide an additional safety valve, that is, a mechanism for automatic adjustment in the economy and would therefore obviate the need to resort periodically to the use of administrative controls on imports and the exchange rate. Import liberalization would, for example, relieve bottlenecks in the key sectors. The present comfortable level of foreign exchange reserves make this an opportune time to consider such liberalization. Similarly, a less restrictive exchange system would increase the role of exchange rates in regulating aggregate demand. Critical steps in this regard include allowing access to swap markets for all current account transactions, increasing the foreign exchange retention ratio to 100 percent, phasing out the foreign exchange plan, progressively reducing the amount of retention quotas that exporters must sell to the state at the prevailing swap rate, replacing the retention quotas with cash retention, and developing an interbank market in foreign exchange.

VII   Conclusions

The purpose of this paper has been to review the evolution of market-oriented reforms in China, assess the impact on the economy, and draw policy implications for framing future reform strategy. A number of factors are pertinent in explaining China's experience with reforms over the past decade and a half. First, the initial macroeconomic conditions were relatively favorable. Growth had been maintained in the pre-reform period—albeit by means of very high investment—while inflation and the balance of payments had been kept under tight control. Moreover, China started its reform with virtually no external debt and was thus able to maximize the benefit of the sustained inflow of foreign resources in support of its reform efforts from official development assistance, commercial borrowing, and foreign direct investment. In the latter regard, China's unique relationship with Hong Kong and Taiwan Province of China has been critical in aiding the flow of physical, financial, and other intangible resources.

Second, the pre-reform political order remained largely intact. Despite internal contention, no fundamental change occurred in the political system, allowing the leadership to concentrate its efforts on economic construction once consensus was reached on the goals and priorities. Third, although any profound change in ownership structures was resisted, the need for market forces to be allowed to operate was accepted. This led to the emergence of such entities as the township and village enterprises and other arrangements that simulated the institutions of a market economy. Fourth, a pragmatism existed in the approach to reform that encouraged experimentation by provinces and local authorities. Indeed, in many cases, reforms consisted of the ratification and generalization of developments that occurred at the provincial level. The evolution of the household responsibility system is a clear example, but other areas, including external trade reform, can also be viewed in this light. Fifth, the very high rates of domestic saving during the reform period were an important source of noninflationary financing of the high rates of investment that were realized.

China has unquestionably made considerable progress in reforming its economy. This reform has contributed to an economic performance marked by rapid growth of output based primarily on improvements in factor productivity; progressive diversification of the economic structure; opening of the economy to the rest of the world; and an impressive export performance. A factor contributing to the impressive growth performance has been regional development policies—an essential element of which has been the progressive decentralization of decision making.

The rapid growth of the economy also reflects in part the dynamism of the nonstate sector comprising the township and village enterprises, the private businesses, and the foreign-funded enterprises. This sector of the economy has been growing at twice the rate of the state-owned sector, and it is projected that by the end of the decade it could account for up to 75 percent of the volume of economic activity. The nonstate sector has contributed to economic reforms in at least two important ways. First, the strong growth in productivity and the concomitant high rate of enterprise saving in this sector has to a large extent compensated for the inefficiencies of the state sector, thus contributing to overall financial stability. Second, the nonstate sector has provided the authorities with a variety of models indicating possible ways to reform traditional institutions and practices so that they function more in accordance with market principles.

The impact of reform is clearest in three areas: the agricultural sector, the related growth of rural enterprises, and the external sector, particularly the growth of exports. Three explanations are possible. First, particularly in agriculture, the extent of the change from pre-existing conditions was sharper and more comprehensive than in other areas. Although formal ownership did not change, the land allocation system was overhauled, incentive structures were considerably strengthened, and many restrictions were removed. Second, perhaps most striking in the TVEs and to a certain extent in the growth of exporting activity, progress was most evident where market forces were allowed the greatest play. Third, in each of these areas, China was in effect resurrecting institutions and skills that had lain dormant for more than a generation. In agriculture, current techniques are based on those used for many generations; all sectors are benefiting from a strong entrepreneurial tradition; and the growth of the coastal regions rests on the comparative advantage of location, a low-cost labor force, and their close relationship with the overseas Chinese diaspora.

Least progress can be observed in those areas in which the approach has been tentative and incomplete, either because of the complexity of the issues involved or because the most determined efforts were made to preserve existing institutions. This feature is most evident in the state enterprise sector where, despite the gradual exposure to market forces, many industries remained subject to mandatory planning and nonmarket pricing. These industries have been protected from market forces by a soft budget constraint motivated by the political goals of maintaining employment opportunities and social stability. Reforms are also incomplete in the financial sector, where progress has been retarded by the slow pace of enterprise reform, the weakness in the fiscal situation, and an inadequate legal and regulatory framework.

A further negative effect of the gradual approach to reforms, however, in which the institutional infrastructure necessary to underpin market-based macroeconomic management has remained underdeveloped, has been a weakening of macroeconomic control manifested in periodic outbreaks of instability characterized by high inflation and/or external imbalances. In responding to these the authorities have had to revert to administrative means of control and to delay reform.

What are the implications for the future reform strategy? It is clear that China has reached the point at which it can no longer avoid a more comprehensive approach. China's leadership has recognized that various sectors of the economy are interconnected and that a broadly based reform strategy on both external and domestic fronts is needed. Reform of the state enterprise sector is crucial, owing to the growing macroeconomic tensions created by its financial needs and the pressure of competition from foreign-funded enterprises and the TVEs. Improving the environment in which the enterprises operate requires comprehensive, simultaneous action in a number of areas, including the price system, enterprise taxation, the financial system, monetary policy, and the social safety net. Due attention should also be paid to the development of a legal and regulatory framework appropriate to a market-based economy. At the same time, China's strategy of opening to the rest of the world implies the need for domestic markets to be more closely linked to world markets, and for the development of China's large domestic market. Finally, the achievement and maintenance of macroeconomic and financial stability primarily through the use of indirect instruments is central to the successful implementation of systemic reforms. This too will be possible only in the context of a comprehensive reform of China's economic institutions.

It is clear that with the renewed political commitment to reforms, China is now well on its way to realizing its full economic potential. How much it actually achieves will depend on the decisiveness and perseverance with which the newly articulated reform strategy is pursued.

Appendix I   Synopsis of Reform from 1978

1978–83	1984–88	1989–Present	Continuing and Possible Future Action

I. External Sector

Exchange System

1978–83	1984–88	1989–Present	Continuing and Possible Future Action
Until 1981, several exchange rates were used for trade transactions between foreign trade corporations (FTCs) and domestic enterprises, depending on item traded. In January 1981, a single exchange rate was established for internal settlement of trade transactions (more depreciated than official rate).	In 1984, exchange rate was unified. Dual exchange system reintroduced in 1986: official rate with de facto peg to U.S. dollar; more flexible rate determined on foreign exchange adjustment centers (FEACs) at which retention quotas are traded; FEAC premium was 53 percent at end-1987 and 80 percent at end-1988.	Official rate devalued in December 1989 (21 percent) and in November 1990 (9 percent); from April 1991, more frequent small adjustments. By mid-1993 the real effective exchange rate (official) was 70 percent more depreciated than in 1980. FEAC premium 17 percent at end-1989, falling gradually to 8 percent at end-1991. Subsequently, premium increased to about 80 percent in 1993 (reflecting market forces).	Eventual unification of the exchange rates. No timetable specified.
Much experimentation with foreign exchange sharing. In 1984 arrangements between local and central governments were formalized. In 1985, some enterprises were given the right to retain a portion of foreign earnings.	Further evolution of complex quota retention system based on location by province and by priority industry. Access to FEACs: initially restricted to foreign-funded enterprises, but in 1988 access was extended to all domestic enterprises with foreign earnings or retention quotas.	System simplified in February 1991, with uniform retention except for mechanical and electrical products. Access gradually extended; by 1990 enterprises could acquire foreign currency for debt service. Individuals allowed to buy and sell at FEAC rates in 1991. Computerized trading introduced in national foreign exchange swap center in Beijing.	Retention and trading of actual foreign exchange to be considered. No timetable specified. Progressive extension of access to the FEACs and integration of trading in all FEACs.

Trade System

1978–83	1984–88	1989–Present	Continuing and Possible Future Action
Foreign trade originally conducted by 12 FTCs, each enjoying monopoly in a particular area, within mandatory trade plan. This system gradually replaced by decentralization, and diminishing role for trade plan. Experimentation with responsibility system for FTCs began. Subsidies on imports and exports.	By mid-1980s foreign trade largely conducted by about 700 FTCs mostly on an agency basis (FTC receives a fee for trading on behalf of domestic enterprises). In 1988, local branches of FTCs became independent and new ones established, bringing total number of FTCs to about 5,000.	Export subsidies abolished in 1991. Rationalization of FTCs begun in 1989 reduces number to about 4,000. By end-1991, over 400 production enterprises could trade directly. Responsibility system extended to all FTCs in 1991.	
Trade licensing: both imports and exports covered by system introduced in 1980. Import tariffs progressively introduced.	Number of licensed imports increased from 45 to 53 in 1988. Exports: number of licensed items reduced from 221 to 159 in 1988. Import tariffs range from 3–150 percent. Periodic adjustments to contain import demand.	Exports subject to license steadily increased to 234 items in 1991. Proportion of trade covered by license (1991): exports—55 percent; imports—40 percent. Tariffs on 40 items reduced in 1991. Harmonized system effective 1992, with reduced duties on 225 items.	Plans announced in 1992 to end two-thirds of import restrictions by 1995, with 16 products removed in 1993.

Synopsis of Reform from 1978 (*continued*)

1978–83	1984–88	1989–Present	Continuing and Possible Future Action

II. Agriculture

Production

Experiments with responsibility system began in 1978. Household responsibility system (HRS) emerges as dominant form by 1983.

Mandatory procurement replaced in 1985 by contracts with households at negotiated prices.

Two-tier management system evolves in many localities: (1) continued HRS framework; and (2) centralized organizations (to provide better services). Some land reverts to the management of the collectives, which lease it out through bidding to maximize efficiency of utilization.

Further evolution with goal of maximizing efficiency of land use.

Prices and Subsidies

Procurement takes place in three tiers: contract (quota), negotiated, and market.

By 1987, market prices dominant at retail level except for some goods such as grain and oil supplied under urban ration.

Support-pricing machinery invoked to guarantee farm incomes in light of large grain harvest. Other prices increased (e.g., cotton).

Some agricultural inputs still supplied at plan or contract prices.
Market prices apply to growing number of retail items; procurement prices increased; subsidies rise.

Subsidies on essential foodstuffs continue to increase sharply.

Large adjustment in urban prices of rationed goods (grain and oil) in May 1991 and April 1992. Rationing abandoned in 1993.
Gradual strengthening of wholesale markets at national, provincial, and local levels.
Grain reserves established to preserve price stability.

National futures trading to be encouraged, to stimulate farmers' supply direct to the market. Further reserves being established for price stability (e.g., in cotton, oils, sugar, wool, rubber).

Food Security

Private interprovincial trade in grain permitted; diminishing role for production targeting.

To counteract stagnating grain output, some intervention increased: more procurement quotas, inputs tied to specified output, and state monopoly on foreign trade in grain.
Grain imports required: national policy to achieve complete autarky.

Some increase in interprovincial barriers during rectification program. From late 1991 these measures reversed for some agricultural products.
Strong production increases in 1990–91 (partly owing to good weather). (Record crop in 1990 of 446 million tons.)

Continued pursuit of complete autarky in grain production. Target of 500 million tons by 2000.

III. Pricing Policy

Enterprise Pricing

Selected SOEs sell a portion of output at negotiated prices on experimental basis.

Dual-track pricing introduced: (1) fixed prices corresponding to plan quotas; (2) guided prices in contracts with state purchasing agencies; (3) market prices for other sales.

Dual-track prices of a large number of commodities were unified, and energy prices adjusted repeatedly.
Ratio of producer goods under fixed/guided/market pricing is down to 45:19:36 in 1991.

Gradual phasing out of the remaining dual-track prices. Timetable not precisely specified.

Synopsis of Reform from 1978 (*continued*)

1978–83	1984–88	1989–Present	Continuing and Possible Future Action

Retail and Other Pricing

Retail prices of most important consumer goods remain under state control.

Some adjustments in administered prices.

Dual-track pricing introduced for many goods. In practice, three tiers of price control exist: state-fixed prices; state-guided prices; market prices (in subtiers): prior approval, guided prices, unrestricted.

By 1988, the three tiers are roughly in the ratio 30:25:45.

Greater market pricing paralleled by the rise of individual and collective retailing (from 10 percent in 1978 to 53 percent in 1987). Efficiency undermined by interprovincial barriers to trade.

Under rectification program price control tightened in 1988–89: (1) fixed and guided prices subject to central (State Council) approval; (2) 50 market prices brought under control.

Relaxation in 1990 and 1991. Prices under State Council reduced to 5. Direct control on market prices eliminated by 1991. "Indirect" measures used to realize price targets: mainly management of inventories of essential commodities.

Large increase in ration prices of grain and edible oil in May 1991 and April 1992, and adjustments to administered prices of goods and services. Rationing abandoned in 1993.

Ratio of fixed/guided/market prices down to 28:17:53 by 1991.

By early 1993, 90 percent of prices "market-determined."

Opening of national metals exchange and wholesale market for nonferrous metals.

Gradual increase in proportion of commodities sold at market prices.

Publication of "price law" to prevent speculation in a more market-oriented environment.

Establishment of wholesale markets, including forward trading.

IV. Enterprises

Ownership Issues

Widespread state ownership, particularly large and medium-sized enterprises. Variously answerable to central, provincial, municipal, or county authorities. Collectives and rural enterprises answer to their local government entity. Private enterprises are small and mainly in retail sector.

Some joint-stock ownership mainly by one enterprise in another, from 1986. Foreign investment through fully owned enterprises and joint ventures.

Securities exchanges open in Shanghai (1990) and Shenzhen (1991).

By end 1991, 6,000 share-issuing companies exist nationwide, of which 69 are listed: 11 are publicly quoted in Shanghai, 6 in Shenzhen. From 1992, foreigners can purchase shares in Chinese enterprises.

More widespread access to securities exchanges to be encouraged.

Conglomerates of SOEs to be established to allow greater autonomy and efficiency. Experiments are under way in 100 of the 3,000 existing groups.

Experiments with joint-stock companies and other forms of shareholding are under way.

State-Owned Enterprises (SOEs)

Experiments with income taxation to replace direct profit transfers to the budget.

Contract responsibility system became formalized for large and medium-sized SOEs. These specify performance targets, supply quotas, and tax obligations.

By 1988, 90 percent of SOEs covered by contracts. First generation of contracts cover three–five years from 1988.

Second generation of contracts similar to first but shorter periods (one–two years) because of financial problems.

Some experiments on new forms of contracting and taxation (see also item VII). Experiment involves 2,000 enterprises in 35 locations.

Twenty measures to revitalize SOEs announced in 1991 being implemented. Increased autonomy of enterprise management, under the new Enterprise Law.

Synopsis of Reform from 1978 (*continued*)

1978–83	1984–88	1989–Present	Continuing and Possible Future Action
Mandatory planning: proportion of output subject to quota declines substantially from the early 1980s. By 1987 about one-third of goods (based on retail sales value) sold under the plan, down from two-thirds in 1980. But many intermediate goods remained largely under direct control, most steel, coal, and almost all petroleum.		"Mutual pledge" system established to protect key SOEs from effects of rectification program: in late 1989, 234 key enterprises received preferences in return for guaranteed sales to the state.	Extent of mandatory planning to be reduced.
Investment: Experimental approach to give SOEs greater autonomy in investment decisions, in line with greater profit retention. Market sanctions: enterprises largely immune from closure.	Responsibility for financing investment largely shifted from the Government to the SOEs (in 1978, 60 percent government financed, in 1987, 20 percent). SOEs allowed access to bank credit and retained earnings. A bankruptcy law formulated in 1986.	In 1989, under the rectification program, many projects were cancelled. Restrictions on investment eased during 1990 and 1991. Bankruptcy law became effective in 1988, but remained almost unused. After 1991, 3,000 inefficient enterprises were merged with others.	Increases planned in key state construction projects. Intention to apply bankruptcy law more widely.
Township and Village Enterprises (TVEs) Existing rural enterprises benefited from increased investment associated with rising agricultural income and availability of surplus labor.	These enterprises designated as TVEs in 1984 being given concessional tax treatment and favorable access to credit.	Credit restrictions under rectification program result in closures, a sharp drop in growth rate, and loss of employment. Credit restrictions eased in second half of 1990. TVE growth accelerates sharply.	Further development of TVEs.
Retail Trade Private traders began to be encouraged in small shops and restaurants.	In 1984–85 about three-fourths of small commercial SOEs were contracted or leased to collectives or individuals.	Some controls were reintroduced under the rectification program.	Privately owned tertiary sector activities to be strongly supported.

V. Wages and Employment

Employment guaranteed in state-owned enterprises and government units. In 1978 bonuses reintroduced, capped at three months' salary. Generally distributed on egalitarian basis, i.e., not based on individual performance. Wages thus include basic wage (centrally determined); component based on level and seniority in the enterprise; and bonuses determined by enterprises or at local level. Wages supplemented by welfare provision: food and rent subsidies; income in kind; other services (e.g., medical and education through the workplace).	Since 1986, recruits to SOEs can be hired under labor contacts (1–10 years' duration). Many exceptions. Cap on bonuses replaced by tax on excessive bonuses.	In 1991, policy announced for next five years, under which uniform wage increases would be phased out. Government would control only the amount of the increase in the total wage bill.	Cast-iron guarantees of jobs to be phased out by the year 2000. Nominal wages to be increased as various reforms implemented, including phasing out of food and rent subsidies. Eventual complete monetization of wages.

Synopsis of Reform from 1978 (*continued*)

1978–83	1984–88	1989–Present	Continuing and Possible Future Action
		VI. Housing	
Pre-1978 system basically unchanged. Housing supplied by municipalities or by work units, involving subeconomic pricing (rent covers one-fifth of operating costs); costs of subsidies and investment borne by enterprises and Government; nonmarket allocation of housing; no housing finance system.	Experimental steps to raise rents (and wage supplements) in a few cities began in 1985.	Focus shifted in 1989 to sale of publicly owned housing, but at steeply discounted prices. Urban rents raised 200–300 percent in early 1992. Experimental housing reform began in Shanghai in 1991. Major features: housing bonds issued to renters; raising rents to cover costs; continued link between workers' housing and their work units.	Over next ten years, gradual reform involving raising rents to cover costs; selling public housing to state employees (state maintains some equity in each house); promotion of financing schemes (including bonds, housing funds, and cooperatives).
		VII. Social Security	
Work units (enterprises and government agencies) responsible for most social security: pensions; job security (a proxy for unemployment benefits); welfare, often including medical and education. Coverage not universal: excludes individuals, contract workers, employees of TVEs, and other rural enterprises.	Experimentation with pension pooling in a few regions began in 1986.	By early 1990, pension pooling among enterprises in 2,200 cities had begun. Contributory pensions are under experimentation in five coastal cities. Experimental unemployment schemes under way in some localities to facilitate implementation of bankruptcy law.	In the medium term: develop a national pension system, particularly for those not now covered; unemployment insurance to have wider coverage; refine medical care arrangements; comprehensive social security schemes in special economic zones.
		VIII. Fiscal Policy	
Resource Sharing (Center/ Provincial Relations) Various forms of revenue sharing: local governments had responsibility for negotiating management contracts, including tax/ profit arrangements with enterprises. Structure favored granting of tax incentives.	Revenue-sharing contracts between central government and provinces started in 1987 or 1988 for three–four year periods. Typically, these involve an agreed base figure and annual rate of increase.	New contracts due to start in 1991 under negotiation. Some experiments with clearer demarcation of center/local resources began in nine provinces in 1992.	Clearer demarcation of center-local resource assignment to become universal. Strengthening central control over fiscal policy.
Budget System/Presentation Consolidated budget; financing flows treated as revenue and expenditure items.	No change in presentation. Rapid growth of extrabudgetary funds (includes enterprises' retained earnings and government units).	Two-tier system announced in 1991 separating current and capital accounts.	Eventual presentation of budget according to international conventions.
Taxation *Enterprise taxation* In 1983, taxation replaces profit transfers from enterprises to Government. Enterprises assume greater responsibility for own funding, own investment.	From 1987, contract responsibility system applied to most medium-sized and large SOEs. Nominal tax payments specified (undermines 55 percent tax rate). Loan repayments are tax deductible. Adjustment tax and other levies imposed on above-contract profits.	New generation of contracts resembles previous generation, but many enterprises seek shorter contracts. Experiments with new system to separate profit and tax: lower tax rates; loan repayments not deductible; contracting on after-tax profits. In 1989, extrabudgetary funds of enterprises subjected to 10 percent levy to preserve government revenue.	Adoption of new tax system. Tax rate for large and medium-sized enterprises would be unified; contracting on after-tax profits; loan amortization nondeductible.

Synopsis of Reform from 1978 (*continued*)

1978–83	1984–88	1989–Present	Continuing and Possible Future Action
Foreign-funded enterprises Wholly owned foreign enterprises taxed at 20–40 percent. Joint ventures taxed at 30 percent. Various incentives (tax holidays, etc.) for new enterprises.	No significant changes. But local governments in SEZs and open coastal cities have considerable discretion in granting additional concessions.	Two tax scales merged in 1991, effective 1992, with tax rate unified at 33 percent.	Unification with domestic enterprise taxation.
Taxes on goods and services Through 1983, indirect taxation of enterprises was conducted through a turnover tax, the consolidated industrial and commercial tax, applied to industrial production, some agricultural sales, imports, retailing, transport, communications, and services.	In 1984 three separate indirect taxes were introduced. Tax rates often set in association with prices to equalize profits, resulting in a wide range of tax rates as follows (1988): value-added taxes—12 rates; product taxes—22 rates; business taxes—4 rates.	Business tax rate change proposed in 1990 and 1991 for revenue purposes; not implemented. VAT extended to petrochemicals.	VAT to be extended to all industries while simplifying and rationalizing the rate structure. Eventual uniform rate after price reform.
Taxes on construction	Tax (at 10 percent) on construction undertaken outside the state investment budget.	In 1991, an investment orientation tax introduced. Variable rates reflect investment priorities.	

IX. Financial Sector

Banking System Monobank system persists. Specialized banks continue to operate in sharply delineated fields.	In 1984, commercial banking activities removed from People's Bank of China, which becomes a central bank. Specialized banks are permitted to engage in commercial banking. In 1986, banks established at provincial level. In 1987, two "universal" banks permitted to compete with existing banks in all forms of business. Networks of urban and rural credit cooperatives supervised by the industrial and agricultural banks. From 1986, all banks allowed to engage in foreign transactions.	Through 1988, a gradual erosion of the sharp demarcation among banks that began to transact outside their own specialization; enterprises allowed to work with more than one bank. Limited competition in interest rates. Under rectification program, specialization reasserted, and competition in interest rates reduced. Competition continued to take the form of the provision of services. Commercial banks expanded their foreign operations.	Strengthening of macroeconomic and supervisory role of the People's Bank as central bank. Reform of payments and clearing systems. Banking laws to be enacted.
Nonbanking Institutions	Trust and investment companies established for loan and equity financing of domestic enterprises; international companies to raise foreign funds. Insurance companies, leasing companies, and financial companies set up, many at provincial level or as part of enterprise groups. Rapid growth of TICs led to restriction of activities in 1988 to permit detailed examination of their operations.	Activities resumed in 1989 with tighter supervision from People's Bank. 375 TICs in operation by end-1991, of which 120 authorized to conduct foreign transactions.	

Synopsis of Reform from 1978 (*concluded*)

1978–83	1984–88	1989–Present	Continuing and Possible Future Action
Financial Markets From 1981 government securities issued through compulsory sales to enterprises and individuals (the former at low interest rates). Enterprises were permitted to issue bonds from 1985. High yields, especially in rural areas. Private enterprises permitted to issue shares from 1982. Shares do not convey ownership. Restrictions imposed in 1987.	Some SOEs issue shares from 1985, which do not convey ownership rights. Some restrictions imposed in 1987. Earmarked bonds for key construction projects began in 1987.	Restrictions placed on interest rates in interbank market (a margin around the People's Bank overnight rate). Secondary markets for treasury bonds opened in major cities. After slow start, secondary market develops rapidly (computerized quotation and trading system established in 1990). Experiments with voluntary placement of government bonds begun in 1991. Securities markets open in Shanghai (December 1990) and Shenzhen (May 1991) (see item III). Experiments with auctioning land use rights accelerated in 1992.	Continue extension of voluntary government bond placement. Development of interbank and money markets, and of new financial instruments. More extensive listing of enterprises on the securities markets and opening markets in other cities. Securities Law to be enacted.
Monetary Policy Monetary policy centers on the credit plan, which is the financial counterpart of the physical plan. Interest rates established by the People's Bank.	Credit plan remains central instrument of monetary policy. De facto decentralization since provincial branches of People's Bank often acquiesce to credit priorities of the provinces. Reserve requirements introduced at high levels when the new banks were established in 1984. In 1985 they were lowered and unified. Banks permitted to adjust lending and deposit rates within margins specified by People's Bank.	Recentralization of decision making to the headquarters of People's Bank. Credit plan abruptly tightened in 1988 in the face of inflation, then relaxed to promote growth and protect SOEs. Some decentralization permitted to provincial branches in adjusting the allocation of plan during 1991. Under rectification program, reserve requirements raised; then "excess reserve" requirements introduced in light of high liquidity and inflation threat. Under rectification program, interest rates raised sharply and interest rate competition largely eliminated. Through 1990 and 1991, interest rates were reduced in three steps. Interest rates increased in 1993.	Introduction of open market operations initially through issuance of short-term bills. Gradual increase in autonomy of banks. Gradual increase in reliance on interest rates, determined through market forces.

Appendix II   Performance of the Provinces: A Statistical Analysis

Some Broad Hypotheses

This appendix presents some statistical evidence bearing on a set of economic hypotheses relating to economic growth across a sample of 28 provinces, autonomous regions, and municipalities. Among the hypotheses investigated are
- the share of state ownership in total production is negatively related to growth performance;
- the degree of government intervention, such as control through production planning, price setting, and sales restrictions, is negatively correlated with provinces' performance;
- the central-provincial fiscal relation plays an important role: provinces with revenue-sharing schedules that mandate only small remittances to the center show stronger growth;
- the degree of openness of a provincial economy to international trade will positively affect its growth;
- foreign capital utilization will have a positive effect on growth;
- a "catch-up" hypothesis: economies with lower initial levels of economic development should grow faster than those with a higher initial level.

The hypotheses that are chosen all yield important policy implications for regional economic growth. It is also important that these hypotheses are testable with available data, but because of data limitations, the exercise is not exhaustive. The regression equation is estimated as follows (t-ratios are in parentheses):

$$GR = 35.13 - 0.20ONS + 6.87LTI$$
$$(7.11) \quad (-6.23) \quad (1.30)$$
$$- \quad 3.18SRR + 3.47FCR \qquad (1)$$
$$(-4.17) \quad (0.72)$$
$$- \quad 2.63log(PNI)$$
$$(-3.62)$$

$$R^2 = 0.856, \qquad N = 28, \qquad DF = 22.$$

In the regression, the real annual average growth rate of per capita industrial output value during 1981–90 is chosen as the dependent variable, GR.[110] ONS is the share of state-owned industrial

output in total industrial output, LTI is the share of light industry's output in total industrial output, SRR is the approximated share of revenue submitted to the center, FCR is the ratio of foreign capital actually utilized to total fixed assets investment, and PNI is the per capita income level in the initial year, 1981. Among the above variables, ONS and LTI are constructed by averaging 1980/81 and 1990 data; SRR and FCR are 1990 data because 1981 data are not available.

The estimated results confirm a number of qualitative observations made in the main text. The model yielded an R^2 of 0.86, implying a surprisingly high explanatory power compared with many cross-section studies on growth. All the explanatory variables have the expected signs and are all statistically significant except FCR (as measured by t-ratios).

The negative coefficient of ONS verifies the hypothesis that higher shares of nonstate ownership promote growth. Although the coefficient of LTI is positive, it is only marginally significant—a result that could be improved by reducing the number of explanatory variables—since there is some evidence of collinearity between ONS and LTI—the correlation coefficient between the two is 0.55. This interpretation is consistent with the fact that slower-growing heavy industries (such as steel, concrete, coal mining, and electricity) are subject to tighter control of production, price setting, and investment approval than light industries. The hypothesis that provinces with favorable revenue-sharing schedules have a stronger potential for growth is also supported by the results, with the coefficient of SRR being significantly negative.

The hypothesized positive effect of high "openness" on growth was not tested in the final form of the equation, because if both the export/GNP ratio and FCR are included in this model, a problem of multicollinearity would arise, leading to insignificant results for both variables. With a correlation coefficient between the two variables as high as 0.77, only one of the two variables is needed, and, statistically, the fourth and fifth hypotheses should be viewed as one. In a number of trials, FCR provided the better fit.

In the full model, the coefficient on FCR had the correct sign but was not significant. To test whether

---

[110]Since industrial production deflators are not available at the provincial level, province-wise retail price indices are used to deflate nominal industrial growth rates.

this stemmed from the number of explanatory variables employed, a simpler specification yielded the following result:

$$GR = \begin{array}{l} 10.30 + 17.79FCR \\ (18.39) \quad (2.72) \\ - 0.0074log(PNI) \\ (-5.28) \end{array} \qquad (2)$$

$$R^2 = 0.55, \quad N = 28, \quad DF = 25.$$

The coefficient on *FCR* became significant at the 1 percent confidence level. This result, to some extent, confirms the efficacy of China's preferential policy for foreign investment and also supports extending the open-door policy to inland provinces.

The final coefficient, for the initial level of per capita income, *PNI*, yielded more robust results in a log-linear specification. The coefficient is negative as the "catch-up" theory expected, a result that may arise from the more rigid industrial structures in the higher-income areas and the greater resistance to change in these more economically important centers.

Impact of Center-Local Fiscal Relations on Guangdong's Performance

This section applies the estimated equation of growth determinants (see above) to calculate the effect on growth if Guangdong had been subjected to one of the most unfavorable revenue-sharing regimes—that between Zhejiang and the center.[111] From 1983 to 1990, the approximate share of net transfers to the center in Guangdong's budgetary revenue ranged from 0.037 to −0.150, whereas the share of Zhejiang ranged from 0.457 to 0.215. The differences between Guangdong and Zhejiang in

---

[111]A variant of the regression equation above is used in estimating the impact of a change in the revenue-sharing schedule on Guangdong's economic growth. The equation is

$$GR = \begin{array}{l} 15.60 - 0.071ONS + 11.43LTI - 1.383\,SRR \\ (16.59) \ (-2.72) \qquad (5.14) \quad (-2.30) \end{array}$$

$$\begin{array}{l} - 2.262\,EXR - 2.658\,IMR \\ (-0.73) \qquad (-0.69) \end{array}$$

$$\begin{array}{l} + 6.522\,FCR - 0.0022\,PNI \\ (1.64) \qquad (-2.78) \end{array}$$

$R^2 = 0.896, N = 28, DF = 21.$

In the regression, the annual average growth rate of per capita national income during 1981–90 is chosen as the dependent variable, *GR*. *ONS* is the share of state-owned industrial output in total industrial output, *SRR* is the approximate share of revenue submitted to the center, *EXR* is the ratio of exports to GNP, *IMR* is the ratio of imports to GNP, *FCR* is the ratio of foreign capital actually utilized to total fixed asset investment, and *PNI* is the per capita income level in the initial year, 1981.

their share of remittances were 0.49 and 0.37 in 1983 and 1990, respectively. Substituting 0.43, an average value of the difference, into the estimated equation (1), it was found that the difference in growth rates arising from the different shares of remittances was 0.59 percentage points. In other words, with Zhejiang's fiscal regime, Guangdong would have had a growth rate of per capita national income that was 0.59 percentage point lower than the actual during 1981–90.

However, this is only a static exercise, which assumes fixed revenue-sharing schedules over time. The conclusion drawn from this may overestimate the effect of fiscal relations on growth. By looking at the change in Guangdong and Zhejiang's share of net transfers to the center, it is clear that although Zhejiang had a higher share of remittance than Guangdong over the whole interval, the share was sharply decreasing for Zhejiang but relatively stable for Guangdong. It suggests that over time there was some leveling out of the benefits arising from differences in fiscal transfers to the center.

Role of Exports in Guangdong

To identify the contribution, or relative importance, of the export sector and the nonexport sector to the high GDP growth rate of Guangdong's economy, the following formula is proposed:

$$GDP_t = NEP_t + EXP_t, \qquad (3)$$

where *NEP* is nonexport domestic output value, and *EXP* is the value of exports. In the empirical analysis, *NEP* is calculated by subtracting *EXP* from *GDP*.

Consider two periods of production in the economy, t and $t+1$. Then the growth rate of GDP can be written as

$$GDP_{t+1}/GDP_t - 1 = (NEP_{t+1} + EXP_{t+1})/ \\ GDP_t - 1$$

$$= (NEP_{t+1}/NEP_t - 1)*\alpha_D \qquad (4) \\ + (EXP_{t+1}/EXP_t - 1)*\alpha_E,$$

where $\alpha_D = NEP_t/GDP_t$, the share of nonexport production in total GDP at t, $\alpha_E = EXP_t/GDP_t$, the share of exports in total GDP at t.

The first term in equation (4) represents the contribution of growth of nonexport production to total GDP growth. It can be understood hypothetically as the growth rate of the economy in the absence of the export sector. The second term measures the contribution of the growth of the export sector to total GDP growth. Using this formula, we calculate the contribution of the export and nonexport sectors both in Guangdong and China as a whole.

The results are shown in Table A1. Between 1978

Table A1. Decomposition of GDP Growth into Export and Nonexport Growth in Guangdong, 1978–90

(In percentages, unless otherwise specified)

	Guangdong			All China		
	GDP	EXP	NEP	GDP	EXP	NEP
Total growth	12.4	20.6	5.0	8.8	17.1	3.3
Weight		0.126	0.873		0.045	0.955
Share of contribution		37.4	62.5		19.9	80.0
Contribution to real annual growth		4.6	7.8		1.7	7.0

Sources: *China Statistical Yearbook, 1991*; and *Guangdong Statistical Yearbook, 1990*.

and 1990, the annual average GDP growth rate in Guangdong was 12.4 percent, 3.6 percentage points higher than the national average. The contribution of export growth to total GDP growth in Guangdong is 37.4 percent, significantly higher than the national average of 19.9 percent. As a result, the part of GDP growth induced by domestic demand in Guangdong is 7.76 percent, only moderately higher than the national average of 7.02 percent. Of the 3.64 percentage point difference between Guang-

dong's GDP growth and the national GDP growth rate, 2.90 percentage points (or 79.6 percent of the total difference) are explained by the difference in export growth, leaving only 0.74 percentage point (or 20.4 percent of the total difference) to be explained by the difference in nonexport production. This suggests that in the absence of a booming export sector, the actual growth rate in Guangdong would not have been significantly higher than the national average.

Bibliography

Beijing Review, 1991 and 1992, various issues.

Bell, Michael, and Kalpana Kochhar, "China: An Evolving Market Economy—A Review of Reform Experience," IMF Working Paper No. 92/89 (Washington: International Monetary Fund, November 1992).

Blejer, Mario I., and Gyorgy Szapary, "The Evolving Role of Fiscal Policy in Centrally Planned Economies Under Reform: The Case of China," IMF Working Paper No. 89/26 (Washington: International Monetary Fund, March 1989).

Blejer, Mario, David Burton, Steven Dunaway, and Gyorgy Szapary, *China: Economic Reform and Macroeconomic Management*, IMF Occasional Paper 76 (Washington: International Monetary Fund, January 1991).

Cheng Chu-yuan, *China's Economic Development: Growth and Structural Change* (Boulder, Colorado: Westview Press, 1982).

China Economic News, Economic Information Agency, Hong Kong, 1991–92, various issues.

Dessi, Roberta, "Household Saving and the Wealth in China: Some Evidence from Survey Data," University of Cambridge, DAE Working Paper No. 9112:1–31 (July 1991).

DRT International, "Taxation in Asia and the Southwest Pacific" (New York, 1990).

Feltenstein, Andrew, David Lebow, and S. van Wijnbergen, "Savings, Commodity Market Rationing, and the Real Rate of Interest in China," *Journal of Money, Credit and Banking*, Vol. 22 (May 1990), pp. 234–52.

Gao Shangquan, and Ye Sen, *China Economic Systems Reform Yearbook* (Beijing: China Reform Publishing House, 1990 and 1991).

Grub, Phillip Donald, and Jian Hai Lin, *Foreign Direct Investment in China* (New York: Quorum Books, 1991).

Guo Wanqing, "The Transformation of Chinese Regional Policy," *Development Policy Review*, Vol. 6 (March 1988), pp. 29–50.

Hamrin, Carol Lee, *China and the Challenge of the Future* (Boulder, Colorado: Westview Press, 1990).

Harding, Harry, *China's Second Revolution: Reform After Mao* (Washington: The Brookings Institution, 1987).

Hishida, Masaharu, "Recent Moves Towards Regional Authority," *China Newsletter*, No. 68 (May–June 1987), pp. 13–18.

Ishikawa, Yuzo, "Regional Economies and Government Finances," *China Newsletter*, No. 83 (November–December 1989), pp. 9–16.

Jiang Zemin, "Accelerating Reform and Opening-Up," Report of the General Secretary of the Central Committee of the Chinese Communist Party to the Fourteenth Party Congress, *Beijing Review*, October 26–November 1, 1992, pp. 10–33.

Khor, Hoe Ee, "China: Macroeconomic Cycles in the 1980s," IMF Working Paper No. 91/85 (Washington: International Monetary Fund, September 1991).

Kueh, Y.Y., "Economic Decentralization and Foreign Trade Expansion in China," in *China's Economic Reforms*, ed. by Joseph C.H. Chai and Chi-keung Leung (Hong Kong: University of Hong Kong, 1987).

Lardy, Nicholas, *Foreign Trade and Economic Reform in China, 1978–1990* (Cambridge, England; New York: Cambridge University Press, 1992).

Li Boxi, Li Yong, and Ma Jun, "China Regional Economic Policy" (unpublished; State Council Development Research Center Report, 1989).

Lin, Justin Yifu, "Rural Reforms and Agricultural Growth in China," *American Economic Review*, Vol. 82 (March 1992), pp. 34–51.

Lyons, Thomas P., "Planning and Interprovincial Coordination in Maoist China," *China Quarterly*, No. 121 (March 1990), pp. 36–60.

Ma Jun, and Zou Gang (1991a), "On the Open Door Policy in China's Border Areas," *Economic Research (Jingji Yanjiu)* (March 1991).

—— (1991b), "Regional Comparative Advantage of Industrial Development in China," *Management World (Guan Li Shi Jie)*, No. 3 (May 1991).

Ma Jun, and Hyung-ki Kim, "System Rigidity and Efficiency Loss: A Comparison Between Chinese State-Owned Enterprises and Town-Village Enterprises" (unpublished; 1992).

Maruya, Toyojiro, "Development of the Guangdong Economy and Its Ties with Beijing," *China Newsletter*, No. 96 (January–February 1992), pp. 2–10.

McKinnon, Ronald, "The Asian Approach to Financial Reforms in Transitional Socialist Economies," paper presented at the Tenth Pacific Basin Central Bank Conference, Beijing, People's Republic of China, October 1992.

Mintz, Jack M., "Corporate Tax Holidays and Investment," *World Bank Economic Review*, Vol. 4 (January 1990), pp. 81–102.

Oksenberg, Michel, and James Tong, "The Evolution of Central-Provincial Fiscal Relations in China, 1971–1984: The Formal System," *China Quarterly*, No. 125 (March 1991), pp. 1–32.

Osborne, Michael, *China's Special Economic Zones* (Paris: Organization for Economic Cooperation and Development, 1986).

Panagariya, Arvind, "Unraveling the Mysteries of China's Foreign Trade Regime: A View from Jiangsu Province," Policy Research Working Paper, WPS 801 (Washington: World Bank, November 1991).

Perkins, Dwight H., "Reforming China's Economic System," *Journal of Economic Literature*, Vol. 26 (June 1988), pp. 601–645.

Qian Yingyi, "Urban and Rural Household Saving in China," *Staff Papers,* International Monetary Fund, Vol. 35 (December 1988), pp. 592–627.

Riskin, Carl, *China's Political Economy: The Quest for Development Since 1949* (New York: Oxford University Press, 1987).

Singh, Inderjit, "China: Industrial Policies for an Economy in Transition," World Bank Discussion Paper No. 143 (Washington: World Bank, 1992).

Tsui Kai Yuen, "China's Regional Inequality, 1952–1985," *Journal of Comparative Economics*, Vol. 15 (March 1991), pp. 1–21.

Wei Yuming, "Bringing the Role of the Coastal Cities into Full Display to Promote Economic and Technological Exchange with Foreign Countries," in *Guide to China's Foreign Economic Relations and Trade: Cities Newly Opened to Foreign Investors*, ed. by Policy Research Department, Ministry of Foreign Economic Relations and Trade (Hong Kong: Economic Information Agency, 1985), pp. 210–12.

Wong, Christine P.W., "Central-Local Relations in an Era of Fiscal Decline: The Paradox of Fiscal Decentralization in Post-Mao China," *China Quarterly*, No. 128 (December 1991), pp. 691–715.

World Bank, *China: Finance and Investment*, A World Bank Country Study (Washington: World Bank, 1988).

—— (1990a), *China: Between Plan and Market*, A World Bank Country Study (Washington: World Bank, 1990).

—— (1990b), *China: Financial Sector Policies and Institutional Development*, A World Bank Country Study (Washington: World Bank, 1990).

—— (1990c), *China: Macroeconomic Stability and Industrial Growth Under Decentralized Socialism*, A World Bank Country Study (Washington: World Bank, 1990).

—— (1992a), *China: Strategies for Reducing Poverty in the 1990s*, A World Bank Country Study (Washington: World Bank, 1992).

—— (1992b), *China: Reform and the Role of the Plan in the 1990s*, A World Bank Country Study (Washington: World Bank, 1992).

—— (1993a), *China: Budgetary Policy and Intergovernmental Relations,* Report No. 11094-CHA (Washington: World Bank, 1993).

—— (1993b), *China: Foreign Trade Reform: Meeting the Challenges of the 1990s*, Report No. 11568-CHA (Washington: World Bank, 1993).

Wu Jinglian, and Lou Jiwei, "China: Intergovernmental Fiscal Relations and Macroeconomic Management" (unpublished; Washington: World Bank, 1991).

Yang Dali, "Patterns of China's Regional Development Strategy," *China Quarterly*, No. 122 (June 1990), pp. 230–57.

Yao Datian, and Luo Zhen, "China to Open in All Directions," *People's Daily*, June 5, 1992.

Zhao Ziyang, "Advance Along the Road of Socialism with Chinese Characteristics," Report of the General Secretary to the Thirteenth Party Congress of the Communist Party of China (October 1987).

Zhou Zhenping, and Ou Yang, "Hainan Establish Joint Office to Approve Foreign Invested Projects," *People's Daily*, May 30, 1992.

Zou Gang, Ma Jun, and Wang Zhigang, "China's Coastal Development Strategy and Pacific Rim Economic Integration," *Journal of East-West Studies,* Vol. 19, No. 2 (1990), pp. 1–61.

Recent Occasional Papers of the International Monetary Fund

83. Economic Reform in Hungary Since 1968, by Anthony R. Boote and Janos Somogyi. 1991.
82. Characteristics of a Successful Exchange Rate System, by Jacob A. Frenkel, Morris Goldstein, and Paul R. Masson. 1991.
81. Currency Convertibility and the Transformation of Centrally Planned Economies, by Joshua E. Greene and Peter Isard. 1991.
80. Domestic Public Debt of Externally Indebted Countries, by Pablo E. Guidotti and Manmohan S. Kumar. 1991.
79. The Mongolian People's Republic: Toward a Market Economy, by Elizabeth Milne, John Leimone, Franek Rozwadowski, and Padej Sukachevin. 1991.
78. Exchange Rate Policy in Developing Countries: Some Analytical Issues, by Bijan B. Aghevli, Mohsin S. Khan, and Peter J. Montiel. 1991.
77. Determinants and Systemic Consequences of International Capital Flows, by Morris Goldstein, Donald J. Mathieson, David Folkerts-Landau, Timothy Lane, J. Saúl Lizondo, and Liliana Rojas-Suárez. 1991.
76. China: Economic Reform and Macroeconomic Management, by Mario Blejer, David Burton, Steven Dunaway, and Gyorgy Szapary. 1991.
75. German Unification: Economic Issues, edited by Leslie Lipschitz and Donogh McDonald. 1990.
74. The Impact of the European Community's Internal Market on the EFTA, by Richard K. Abrams, Peter K. Cornelius, Per L. Hedfors, and Gunnar Tersman. 1990.
73. The European Monetary System: Developments and Perspectives, by Horst Ungerer, Jouko J. Hauvonen, Augusto Lopez-Claros, and Thomas Mayer. 1990.
72. The Czech and Slovak Federal Republic: An Economy in Transition, by Jim Prust and an IMF Staff Team. 1990.
71. MULTIMOD Mark II: A Revised and Extended Model, by Paul Masson, Steven Symansky, and Guy Meredith. 1990.
70. The Conduct of Monetary Policy in the Major Industrial Countries: Instruments and Operating Procedures, by Dallas S. Batten, Michael P. Blackwell, In-Su Kim, Simon E. Nocera, and Yuzuru Ozeki. 1990.
69. International Comparisons of Government Expenditure Revisited: The Developing Countries, 1975–86, by Peter S. Heller and Jack Diamond. 1990.
68. Debt Reduction and Economic Activity, by Michael P. Dooley, David Folkerts-Landau, Richard D. Haas, Steven A. Symansky, and Ralph W. Tryon. 1990.
67. The Role of National Saving in the World Economy: Recent Trends and Prospects, by Bijan B. Aghevli, James M. Boughton, Peter J. Montiel, Delano Villanueva, and Geoffrey Woglom. 1990.
66. The European Monetary System in the Context of the Integration of European Financial Markets, by David Folkerts-Landau and Donald J. Mathieson. 1989.
65. Managing Financial Risks in Indebted Developing Countries, by Donald J. Mathieson, David Folkerts-Landau, Timothy Lane, and Iqbal Zaidi. 1989.
64. The Federal Republic of Germany: Adjustment in a Surplus Country, by Leslie Lipschitz, Jeroen Kremers, Thomas Mayer, and Donogh McDonald. 1989.
63. Issues and Developments in International Trade Policy, by Margaret Kelly, Naheed Kirmani, Miranda Xafa, Clemens Boonekamp, and Peter Winglee. 1988.
62. The Common Agricultural Policy of the European Community: Principles and Consequences, by Julius Rosenblatt, Thomas Mayer, Kasper Bartholdy, Dimitrios Demekas, Sanjeev Gupta, and Leslie Lipschitz. 1988.
61. Policy Coordination in the European Monetary System. Part I: The European Monetary System: A Balance Between Rules and Discretion, by Manuel Guitián. Part II: Monetary Coordination Within the European Monetary System: Is There a Rule? by Massimo Russo and Giuseppe Tullio. 1988.

Note: For information on the title and availability of Occasional Papers not listed, please consult the IMF *Publications Catalog* or contact IMF Publication Services.